SIN CITY
RETRIBUTION

STOLEN STEEL

RICK HART

SIN CITY RETRIBUTION: STOLEN STEEL

1405 SW 6th Avenue • Ocala, Florida 34471 • Phone 352-622-1825 • Fax 352-622-1875
Website: www.atlantic-pub.com • Email: sales@atlantic-pub.com
SAN Number: 268-1250

Library of Congress Cataloging-in-Publication Data

Names: Hart, Rick, 1948- author.
Title: Sin City retribution : stolen steel / by Rick Hart.
Description: Ocala, Florida : Atlantic Publishing Group, 2019.
Identifiers: LCCN 2018053344 (print) | LCCN 2019000579 (ebook) | ISBN 9781620236208 (ebook) | ISBN 9781620236192 (pbk.)
Subjects: LCSH: Hart, Rick, 1948—-Fiction. | Motorcycle gangs—Fiction. | Motorcycle clubs—Fiction. | GSAFD: Autobiographical fiction.
Classification: LCC PS3608.A7867 (ebook) | LCC PS3608.A7867 S56 2019 (print) | DDC 813/.6—dc23
LC record available at https://lccn.loc.gov/2018053344

Printed in the United States

PROJECT MANAGER: Katie Cline
INTERIOR LAYOUT AND JACKET DESIGN: Nicole Sturk

Over the years, we have adopted a number of dogs from rescues and shelters. First there was Bear and after he passed, Ginger and Scout. Now, we have Kira, another rescue. They have brought immense joy and love not just into our lives, but into the lives of all who met them.

We want you to know a portion of the profits of this book will be donated in Bear, Ginger and Scout's memory to local animal shelters, parks, conservation organizations, and other individuals and nonprofit organizations in need of assistance.

– Douglas & Sherri Brown,
President & Vice-President of Atlantic Publishing

TABLE OF CONTENTS

1975

CHAPTER I

VALLEY OF FIRE

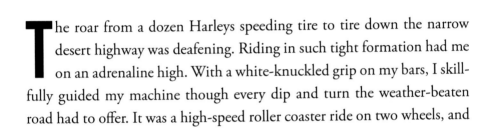

The roar from a dozen Harleys speeding tire to tire down the narrow desert highway was deafening. Riding in such tight formation had me on an adrenaline high. With a white-knuckled grip on my bars, I skillfully guided my machine though every dip and turn the weather-beaten road had to offer. It was a high-speed roller coaster ride on two wheels, and one mistake would send the pack down like a row of dominoes.

I was at the front of the group next to Stroker. We down-shifted through the gears, slowing our motors as we approached the crossroads ahead. As we came to a stop, I looked back for Baby Huey. Huey was the club president, and he was nowhere in sight.

He should have been leading the pack, but his bike had been running a little rough. He thought it would be in his best interest to not be at the head of a speeding pack of bikes if his motor decided to unexpectedly stall.

We had been so focused on the road ahead, we didn't realize we were missing four of our bros. We looked at each other wondering if anyone had an answer, but everyone came up empty.

My first thought was that Baby Huey's scoot had broken down somewhere behind us.

As the bikes idled between our legs, we slowly muscled them to the side of the road and waited. Stroker, a 6-foot-4 giant of a man with long blond hair and a beard to match, turned off his machine and signaled for the rest of us to do the same by slicing his hand under his neck. The V-Twins died one by one and soon a quiet desert breeze became apparent. Everyone stared in the direction from which we had traveled, struggling to hear even a faint sound of Harleys in the distance. But the air was silent.

Everyone stepped off their ride and gathered together in the center of the crossroads. My eyes slowly drifted from the road behind us to the red sandstone rock formations all around. It was a bright, sunny day with a cloudless, deep blue sky in the area that was aptly called the Valley of Fire. It was 108 degrees and still rising as the sun rose higher overhead.

I wiped the sweat from my brow as we waited impatiently. I could feel the heat from the road penetrating the soles of my boots, and shade was nowhere to be found.

"It's too damn hot standing here doing nothing," yelled Stroker. "Hiney, you and Lance were bringing up the rear — didn't you notice that no one was behind you?"

"I was doing good to just keep up with you and Turk," Hiney answered back. "I wasn't taking my eyes off the road for no one."

Stroker looked over at Lance, our newest and youngest member. Stroker just shook his head and turned away. He knew Lance didn't have a clue where the others were, just by the expression on his face.

"Hey man," Norton reasoned, "why don't we send a couple guys to go back and find them while the rest of us head on in to Overton? I need a drink, man."

"Are you out of your damn mind?" yelled Stroker. "No one's leaving until we find out what happened to them."

"Well, damn it, Stroker," said Norton. "We need to do something quick."

"Norton's right," I said. "We need to find them, and we need to find them now. Let's get this show on the road."

I threw my leg over my 1968 Harley Shovelhead and twisted the ignition switch on. After pumping the pedal twice, I kicked down hard, and my engine roared to life. I felt the heat from the engine rise between my legs. That same uncomfortable but familiar burning sensation I felt on my inner thighs is the reason most bikers walk bow-legged.

The still desert air was once again filled with the thunder of our motors as we slowly turned our bikes around and opened them up.

We throttled hard through each gear and retraced our route through the Valley of Fire. *What the hell happened to them? I can't believe we lost them.* I hated to backtrack in this heat, but we couldn't leave our bros behind.

I thought we would come upon them around each corner and over every blind hill. I pushed my motorcycle harder and harder, and at times, beyond my comfort zone.

My thirst for a cold beer made me take chances through these curves I normally wouldn't have.

I was just getting into the groove of my bike's speed when we topped a steep crest and suddenly found ourselves on top of them. We slammed on our brakes and fishtailed past our bros. My rear wheel locked up as my Harley began to slide at over 60 miles per hour. Out of the corner of my eye, I saw the front tire of Rotten Ralph's bike come up on my right side. My heart was pumping through my chest. *Don't hit me. Don't hit me. Don't hit me.* His old panhead came sliding past me, narrowly missing my scoot.

In our frenzy to find our friends, we threw common sense out the window and almost paid a huge price. When we all finally came to a stop, we looked around at each other to make sure everyone was all right.

I looked over my shoulder and on down the road behind us. The small group that had gone MIA was standing in the road, staring at us in disbelief.

Baby Huey, Spider, and Grube were standing wide-eyed with Lil' Dave and his ol' lady, Chris, sitting in their shadows. All their attention was now focused on us.

We turned our bikes around and idled over to the side of the road. I shut off my scoot and kicked out my side stand as Baby Huey approached me. He was not happy.

"What the fuck are you and Stroker trying to do — kill everyone? What the hell was that all about?" he shouted.

"What are you talking about, man?" I asked. "We came back to see what the hell happened to you guys."

"Well, if you two weren't too busy driving like maniacs in the first place, you would have already known what happened. You need to keep your head out of your ass while you're leading the club out on the open road!"

"Damn it, Huey," I yelled. "I don't need a lesson on how to ride my Harley. What the fuck happened to you guys?"

"Lil' Dave and his ol' lady lost it on the hill back there and went off the road."

Baby Huey said this way too calmly for my liking. I leaned to peer around Huey to see if I could spot Lil' Dave.

Turning back to Huey, I asked, "Are they all right?"

"Yeah," Huey said. "Just some scratches and bleeding — nothing serious."

Judging from his tone and his crossed arms, he was being put out by all this. Fine by me — I was tired of asking questions and getting half-assed answers. I needed to go see for myself.

I climbed off my scoot and headed over to the edge of the road where Lil' Dave and Chris were sitting. The desert had shown them no mercy when they traded road for rock and sand. I knelt on one knee to get a better look at the two of them. My first thought was that we needed a truck to get them and their bike to Vegas, which was some 40 miles back in the scorching heat.

"What happened, Dave?"

"Man, I traded my stock glide front end for that fucking 12-inch over springer, and it couldn't handle the speed over these damn hills. When I topped that one back there," he said, jabbing his thick thumb over his shoulder, "the weight of my ol' lady on the back took it on up in the air. I felt the front end lift off the ground. Coming down on the other side of the hill, I was doing a full-fledged wheelie! Thank God, we didn't go all the way over. The bike dropped forward, and the front end slammed down onto the pavement. The springer bounced back up and off the road we went." The whole time he spoke, he was animating the action with his hands.

Lil' Dave paused a moment and ran his hand over his girl's face. He carefully brushed her hair back to reveal the bloody knots on her forehead from her tumble off the bike. Her tank top had offered no protection from the blacktop, evident from the road rash on her upper right shoulder.

"I'm just glad you're okay, baby."

Lil' Dave leaned forward and planted a gentle kiss on her forehead.

"I'm so sore and thirsty," Chris said. "I really need something to drink, Davey."

"I know, baby. I know," Lil' Dave said, looking up at me for an answer.

"Is your bike drivable?" I asked.

"Really don't know, Turk. Haven't checked her out yet."

"Sit tight, man. I'll have Hiney look at it for you." I patted him on the back and stood up.

"Thanks, Turk."

I stood up and looked through the crowd for Hiney. I finally spotted him standing in the shade of a cactus talking to Baron.

"Hiney, see if you can start Dave's bike or if it's even drivable."

"I just checked it," Hiney said. "Front tire's flat."

I looked around for Baby Huey and found him sitting sidesaddle on his scoot, casually talking to Stroker.

"Hey, what the hell is the plan?" I asked.

"The plan," Huey shouted back, "is that we should have been in Overton by now."

"Oh great! That's it? That's all you've got?"

"Well, tell me, Turk," he yelled. "What's *your* plan?"

"Oh, so now *I'm* running the show. Is that it?" We were getting more and more heated under the scorching desert sun.

Baby Huey stood up from his bike, trying to intimidate me with his bulk. He might have been able to freak most people out, but not me.

I was a black belt in Tae Kwon Do and had trained far too long and hard to worry about any man, no matter the size. I'm not saying I was bad, but the bad didn't want any part of me.

"What's your problem, Turk? You don't like the way I run things around here?"

Huey started toward me with a snarl on his mug, and I knew he wouldn't stop until he was in my face.

"Well, now that you bring it up, no. I don't," I replied with steely resoluteness. "Why the hell didn't you send someone ahead to get us after the accident? We had no idea what had happened to you guys. We had to blindly find our way back here."

"Yeah? Well, your so-called blind backtracking almost caused another accident! Maybe *you* weren't thinking either, Turk. Could that be possible?" He had made it over to where I stood and was leaning menacingly over me. "We were too busy with Lil' Dave and Chris," Huey yelled. "We were taking care of the business at hand!"

"Don't you think sending one rider back to find us would have brought the club together on this? Or didn't *you* think at all?"

"Don't let the fact that you're the club's Sgt. at Arms go to your head, Turk. I'm not going to put up with your bullshit today." His voice had lowered to a dangerous growl.

"One of my jobs is to make sure the club members are safe," I said. "That's why I'm in this position. I guess it looks like I'll have to pick up your slack, too."

For Baby Huey, the time for talking was over. I saw it coming before he even swung. I ducked just as his powerful right hook whizzed over my head. When I came up, I jammed my fist hard between his legs with an upper cut.

His legs buckled for just a few seconds, but that was all the time I needed. I grabbed his left leg and pulled it up waist high.

Huey grabbed at my cut-off jean jacket for balance as I walked him backwards. We stumbled off the road unexpectedly, and we went rolling down the embankment to an abrupt landing at the bottom. When we came to our feet, we were both swinging.

I won't say our timing was bad, but as we were each busy trying to knock the other's head off, a Nevada Highway Patrol unit rolled up.

The officer saw the crowd gathered on the side of the road in the middle of nowhere and decided to investigate. Why were a dozen or so motorcycles parked all over the road? And more so, why was the shady crew that owned them all staring down into a ditch?

"What the hell is going on here?" he barked as he stepped from his patrol car.

Everyone was so engrossed in the brawl below that they hadn't even heard him roll up. Being caught with their pants down was a very unusual occurrence for this bunch. Rotten Ralph stepped away from the edge and pointed to the wrecked bike.

"One of our bros went down, man!" he said, trying his best to sound desperate. "Can you radio in for a tow truck?"

To divert the cop's attention away from the brawl going on in the gully, some 15 feet below the highway's surface, Rotten Ralph tried to steer the officer towards his car and make a call for help.

The cop wasn't buying it. He grew a bit more cautious when he realized that he'd pulled up to a whole lot more than a group of motorcycle enthusiasts.

"What's so interesting down there?"

"That's just where my buddy crashed his scoot, man," answered Rotten Ralph. "Seriously, can you call a truck?"

"Really?" the cop said, his voice dripping with disbelief. "Maybe I'll just have a look myself."

The patrolman side stepped Ralph and walked over to look over the edge. When he saw the tussle going on at the bottom of the pit, he took a little leap back. His hand made its way to the pistol on his belt, his finger releasing the holster snap over the hammer. He started giving the club a good long once over. As he regained his composure, he pointed to the embankment.

"Someone go down and break those two up."

"You break them up," said Spider incredulously. "Isn't that your job?"

"You want me to do it?" said the officer with a laugh in his voice. "Fine!"

He walked to the edge and looked over. All he saw was two, long-haired, bearded bikers smashing each other around. It wasn't a pretty sight for the average Joe to witness. He drew his gun, and with both hands wrapped firmly around the .357 magnum, he took careful aim.

I was totally unaware of the pistol aimed at my head as I spit blood and dirt into the gravel at Baby Huey's feet. He was throwing fists left and right, and several managed to land. Huey was a combat vet from Vietnam and a seasoned street fighter. Even with all my martial arts training, I had my hands full with this guy.

Huey threw a hard right to my head, and its power went right through my defenses and into my jaw.

I staggered back a few steps, but when I regained my balance, I threw a roundhouse kick of my own into his outer thigh.

I followed that with a front snap kick straight to his gut, which put him on his ass.

"Fuck you and your karate bullshit!" Huey yelled from the dirt. "That all you got?"

Baby Huey scrambled to his feet and bum rushed me. He was swinging wildly, and it was all I could do to avoid this deadly windmill of strikes. My arms were really taking a beating as I tried to ward off his attacks. This had to stop. I timed it out and pushed his next punch away from me, swinging behind him. I jumped up onto his back and tried to put the beast into a chokehold, but he wrenched me away and threw me into the dirt.

Once the wind returned to me, I found myself staring up at a fuming giant.

Damn it, I thought. It seemed like, no matter how hard I hit him, nothing made a dent. I knew I had the ability to do some major physical damage to him, but I didn't want to hurt Huey that way. No matter how mad I got, I had to fight him hard enough to put him down, but not so hard that he went down for good.

I quickly rolled to my side and side kicked him in the shin, just below the knee.

"Ouch! You son of a bitch!" Huey yelled in pain, as he hobbled back, grabbing for his leg.

That's all the time I needed to get back to my feet. I stepped forward and gave him one of my best hooks. Any normal man would've been on his back, out cold, but not Huey. He just staggered back a few paces.

He was still a little off balance when my right foot connected with his belly, finally putting him on his ass. I stood over him but not with any pride. Hell, I wanted this shit over with. We were in a lava pit of burning sand and dried up tumbleweed, and it was taking its toll on me. *This needs to end*, I thought as Huey rose to his feet.

As the hammer on the silver pistol clicked into position, Stroker barreled toward the officer. Instinctively, the cop swung the gun in Stroker's direction.

"Whoa! Whoa! Whoa!" said Stroker, as he slid to a halt, waving his arms in surrender. "Calm down! I got this! Relax, man, I got this!"

Stroker made his way down the sandy cliff to where we were still exchanging blows.

We were so focused on each other that we were completely unaware of the police issue aimed at our heads.

Stroker was shortly followed down the embankment by Grube and Baron, and the three of them tackled us to the ground.

"It's over dudes!" Stroker yelled. "The Man's up there, and he has his revolver aimed at you two assholes."

"You've got to be fucking kidding me!" I said, spitting blood and grit from my dry mouth. "What's that all about?"

My body was overcome by exhaustion. I laid looking up at the edge of the road for the cop and didn't feel like moving anytime soon. I was thirsty and the dryness in my throat was aching for a beer.

"What's he doing here?" Huey asked.

"Be cool, man. He just rolled by, but we need him to call a tow truck," Stroker explained. "He wants you two up on the road, now."

Baby Huey and I were both bruised and exhausted from our scuffle, so neither one of us was ready to climb that steep hill back up to the road.

The sand on the embankment was loose and hot, and scaling that desert wall was going to take quite a bit of effort on our part.

That being said, the gun muzzled at our heads was a strong motivator to get topside. I looked over at Huey and had to smile.

"You ready for this?"

"What the hell could possibly happen next?" asked Huey. "Let's get our asses up there."

We slowly crawled our way up the side of the embankment. Once we reached the top, we leaned over our knees gasping for air as everyone looked on.

"All right you two, who hit who first?" the officer shouted. "Who started the fight?"

He wasn't quite sure if it was safe to put the weapon away, faced with two rather scary-looking bikers, so he opted to keep it leveled at the ground in our direction.

He kept looking over his shoulder at his cruiser, the only connection with the outside world. His radio was there, but it was some 50 feet behind him.

I walked over and rested my arm over Huey's shoulders.

"What fight?" I asked with an innocent grin. "I was just showing my buddy here some basic self-defense techniques."

"Is that right?" The cop furrowed his brow, knowing it was all a crock of shit. "How about you?" he said, looking up at Baby Huey.

"Like the man said, officer. We were just having a little morning workout."

Huey reached under my arm and picked me up at the waist. With a loud grunt, he tossed me over his shoulder and carried me to my bike, slamming me down beside it.

"Now, you stay here and be a good boy," Huey said as if to a 5-year-old. He patted me on top of my head. "Don't get any ideas about giving the nice policeman a hard time, you hear?"

The tension was instantly cut by a roar of laughter from the rest of our bros. Everyone was laughing — except for the patrolman, that is.

"All right, that's it!" he shouted. "I want all of you off my road, now!"

He holstered his weapon but kept a hand hovering over the holster as he slowly walked back to his car. Stroker ran over and stopped him just before he closed his door.

"Wait man, what about that tow truck?" he said in desperation, his laughter gone. "We can't go anywhere until we get help."

The cop hesitated, but sighed and said, "Yeah, I can do that." He looked put out. "The sooner you're off my road the better."

He got on his radio and had a tow truck dispatched to our location. He leaned out the door and yelled at Stroker, who was standing in front of his car.

"It'll be about two, maybe three hours at least for the driver to get here. That's the best he could do," he said with mock sympathy. "Make yourselves comfortable," he added with a smirk. "It's gonna be a while."

Without waiting for an answer, the officer slammed his door and sped off in a cloud of dust.

Within minutes, we could feel the heat burning through our clothes. I slid my arms out of my cut-off jacket and pulled it over my head like a hood for protection from the intense and ever-rising sun. It was really looking bad for us and that damn cop knew we'd be in trouble without any water.

Baby Huey stuck his finger in Stroker's face.

"Get your ass on your scoot, and go get us something to drink! Take Rotten Ralph and Grube with you. I need you back yesterday!"

"I'm on it, man!" Stroker said as he ran over to his bike, yelling at the other two members to get a move on. The three bikes roared to life, and as the Harleys pulled away, a little relief filled my body. Within minutes, the desert fell silent again. I looked up and saw Huey wiping sweat and grit from his forehead.

"Good call, Huey," I said. "You all right?"

"Hell yeah, I'm fine!" he said. "If you have any more problems with my way of doing things, just let me know."

He walked over and slung his arm around my neck in a headlock and squeezed. I slipped out of his chokehold, stepping away.

"You can rest assured that you'll be the first to know. And don't make me throw you back into that ditch," I added with a grin. "The cops aren't here to save you this time!"

"Save *me*?" he laughed.

Our hands flew together with a loud smack, as they gripped tightly together in a high-five handshake. We gave each other a well deserved hug of brotherly love and a hard slap on the back.

I looked over at my 7-year-old Harley and thought about the long ride back to town. I wished I could just jump on her and jam home, but you simply don't leave a brother behind.

As the sun settled into it's high-noon position over the Valley of Fire, all hope of finding shade was lost. I slumped down beside my bike and pulled my cut back over my head.

Bike clubs proudly fly their colors (or cuts) identifying themselves with the club's name on the back of a denim or leather sleeveless vest. To us, our cuts were sacred. They were worth fighting and, if need be, dying for.

Time seemed to stand still as we waited in the scorching, dusty desert for help to arrive. I impatiently strained to hear any sound of returning Harleys breaking the silence, but I could hear nothing but my own heart thudding heavily through my chest from dehydration.

I looked over my shoulder at my scoot, and my mind started to drift. I had just bought her a few months back from a friend of mine named Cecil. He had just finished putting together this nice 1968 FLH and was about ready to spend the summer riding it until I saw her.

I had stopped by his house one night to talk to him about painting my Sportster tank when I laid eyes on his winter project. I fell instantly in love.

It had a gunmetal gray paint job that was fit for a custom bike show. The stock wide glide front end was stripped down and completely chromed with a 21-inch narrow front tire. It still had the stock handlebars with the suicide throttle, which acts like cruise control because you have to physically twist it on and off.

The rear end was lowered with a pair of shortened shocks with a bobbed rear fender, and the banana seat was hard but looked awesome. The finishing touch was the chromed-out rebuilt 74-cubic inch Shovelhead mill. I had to ask if he would consider selling her.

"Hell no, man," Cecil replied. "I just got her ready for the summer!"

"Well, say you *were* going to sell her — what do you think she's worth?"

"You know what, Turk? If you want this ride, it'll cost you $2,400."

"Are you kidding me?! I could buy a brand new 1975 Harley for that!"

"That's right," Cecil said with a smile and a shrug. "Like I said, she's not for sale."

I didn't mention the bike again that night, but, believe me, the wheels were turning in my mind. As I rode my '72 XLH Sportster home that night, I couldn't get Cecil's bike out of my mind. By morning, I had decided to sell my Sportster and raise enough money to buy Cecil's bike.

It turned out to be much easier to sell my bike than I had thought. A co-worker at the Mint Hotel wanted to buy it.

Two days later, I was signing the title over to my assistant manager in valet. I was still about $700 shy, but that was no problem.

Where there's a will, there's a way. A little paperwork at the bank and I was set.

It was five nights later when I walked back into Cecil's garage. I had called him earlier and told him I needed to stop by and show him something.

Cecil was squatting beside the bike when I walked in. He looked up over his shoulder and smiled.

"What's up, Turk?"

"I told you I had something to show you. Check it out."

I pulled out a white envelope, opened it and slowly slid out 24 $100 bills. Cecil's eyes widened as I fanned them out.

"$2,400? That's what you said, right?" I asked, grinning.

Cecil slowly took the money from my hands and stared at it dazedly for a moment.

"Turk, you son of a bitch!" Cecil shook his head in disbelief. "Damn it! Now I have to start all over building another bike!"

"Yeah," I slapped him on the back, "but now you have the cash to build an even better one."

Secretly, I didn't think a better bike than this could even exist. I just said it to make him feel better about our deal.

Riding home on my first big twin was a treat. This '68 Shovelhead rode so much better than my '72 Sportster. I was in absolute heaven. She was truly perfect.

I blinked and was back, slowly baking in the Valley of Fire. I tried to swallow, but my mouth was so dry that I gagged. I looked around at my bros and could see that they were no better off.

No one spoke as our throats grew more cracked and raspy by the second. It had to be over 112 degrees now.

Hiney and Lance were still checking out Lil' Dave's bike, thinking it may be still roadworthy, but that was a lost cause. Even if they *could* somehow get her to start, the front tire was completely flat.

I thought about how good a cold beer would taste right now and how Stroker and the boys would probably down a few before they headed back for us. I should have gone with them, but everyone else was probably thinking the same thing.

Suddenly, I heard a faint noise in the distance, and my heart jumped through my chest. Could it be Stroker and the boys already? As it got louder I realized that the sound was coming from the opposite direction from which the bikes would be returning. I looked to the west and could make out a black pickup pulling a boat slowly making its way toward us.

No way we're that lucky, I thought.

I quickly jumped to my feet and my head started spinning immediately. I took two steps back and almost tripped over my bike.

"Turk!" Baby Huey yelled. "We gotta stop that truck!"

"No shit!" I said. "Let's get out in the middle of the road so he has to stop!"

I looked over at Baron, who was removing a gun from his inner vest pocket.

"What the fuck, Baron?!" I yelled. "Put that shit away!"

"What if he doesn't stop, Turk? What then?"

"He sure as hell won't stop if he sees a gun! Lose it — now!"

"Huey! What do you say?" Baron yelled, still holding his gun at the ready.

"Damn it, Baron!" Huey said, while running into the middle of the street. "Turk's right. If that guy sees a gun, of course he won't stop!"

Baron reluctantly stuffed the gun in the rear of his pants. I saw that he had not put it back into his inner vest pocket, but I left well enough alone. The three of us were in the road, watching as the truck came closer. As he approached, he blasted his horn for us to get out of the way, but that wasn't going to happen. I guess you could say we were playing chicken, and it didn't look like the driver wanted to lose.

At the last minute, Baron pulled his gun out from its hiding place, and with both hands gripping the pistol, he took steady aim.

The driver slammed on the brakes and slid right up to where Baron could almost touch the grill with the tip of his pistol. As it was, the driver kept his windows rolled up and the doors locked.

If it had been me driving, I would have just run Baron over. I walked over to the driver's door, thinking mainly of how screwed I'd be if the driver also had a gun.

"Hey, man," I yelled through the tinted window. "We need your help!"

I held my hands out to my side to show the driver I was unarmed. We needed to talk to him, but the engine kept running. I looked over at Baron, who now had his forearms propped on the hood of the truck, taking careful aim at the driver.

"Baron, knock it off!"

He put the gun back into his inner vest pocket and held his arms out to his side with a devious smile. I was so relieved he didn't give me a hard time. I didn't want this to turn into an armed robbery.

"Hey man, it's cool," Baron said, shrugging off the fact that he had just held a stranger at gunpoint.

I looked back at the driver's side window and strained to see though the glass. Who was driving and how many people were in there?

I figured the driver's eyes were glued on Baron, so I needed to get his attention.

"Hey, buddy!" I yelled, as I banged on the driver's window. "We need your help! "

Still, no budge from the driver to acknowledge us. I was trying not to act desperate, but my thirst was about to drive me mad. I visualized in my mind just smashing out the window, but suddenly, the hum of a powered window lowering caught my attention.

"Man, are we glad to see you," I said eagerly with a big smile. "Do you have anything to drink? We've been stuck out here for a while, and we seriously need something to drink."

The driver looked me over then looked over at everyone gathered on the side of the road.

"What are you guys doing out here in the heat?" asked the driver.

"One of our bros had an accident, and we're waiting on a tow truck. it's taking forever, and the heat is really getting to us."

I reached back into my back pocket and pulled out my wallet. I opened it and counted out my cash.

"Look, I have some money here. We'll pay for what you can spare. I know you must have a cooler back there, right?"

Baby Huey and Baron kept their distance from the truck, but remained in the center of the road, just in case he decided to bolt.

I watched as the driver checked out the wrecked bike on the side of the road then looked over at his friend, who was in the passenger's seat. After a few words were spoken between them, the driver looked back down at me.

"Anybody hurt?" he asked. "We're headed for Overton, and we could send some help."

"Thanks, but no. We have a tow truck coming. What we need is something to drink. Come on man, I know you have something back there."

"Well, we do have a cooler in the back of the truck. I guess we could spare a few."

The two truckers jumped out of the cab and escorted us the rear truck bed. He dropped the tailgate with a loud bang and slid the blue cooler onto it. Pulling off the white lid, we saw the mother lode. There was about a case of beer floating in a bed of precious ice and water. *That's it. He's not leaving with this cooler.*

"We're buying the whole cooler from you," I yelled, as I pulled out the $30 from my wallet.

I wasn't going to take no for an answer.

I shoved the money toward him and waited. The driver hesitated for a moment, shaking his head no. I knew we had to have looked like a pack of madmen as he stared at his partner. His partner was nodding in approval as he looked around at us in a bit of panic.

"Do it, Jeff," said his partner. "We can buy more beer in Overton."

I saw that the driver, Jeff, didn't really want to lose his cooler but he finally reached for the money.

"Sure," he said. "Glad we could help."

He sounded a little disappointed, but that wasn't my problem. The truckers took a wide step back, and the cooler was officially ours.

In seconds, Baby Huey and Baron had the cooler off the truck.

The three of us screamed at everyone as we trotted across the blistering, two-lane asphalt highway, ice chest in tow.

The black truck sped off into the far distance as we dove into the cooler like a pack of wolves feeding on its prey. Everyone splashed cold water on their necks and faces, while laughing and guzzling the cold, life-giving beer.

There's little in this world better than the taste of an ice-cold beer, but nothing has ever compared to the taste of that beer in the Valley of Fire.

CHAPTER 2

LANCE

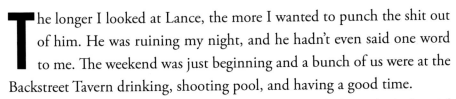

The longer I looked at Lance, the more I wanted to punch the shit out of him. He was ruining my night, and he hadn't even said one word to me. The weekend was just beginning and a bunch of us were at the Backstreet Tavern drinking, shooting pool, and having a good time.

The Backstreet Tavern was our favorite watering hole in the industrial area by the railroad tracks. It was off the beaten path, and we liked it that way. We knew the owner and pretty much had free run of the place.

It was the weekend after our run in the Valley of Fire, and we were hanging out shooting pool and unwinding a bit.

I peered into my pint glass and remembered the look on Stroker's face when he, Grube, and Rotten Ralph returned with a case of beer, thinking they were going to save our asses, just to find us dancing around in the road.

The tow truck did finally arrive, and the party continued at Lil' Mike's house till the early morning.

We had another big run planned tomorrow morning, this time to Ash Springs, so we were all in good spirits. Everyone, that is, except for Lance. He seemed a bit on edge as he twisted his drink in circles on the bar. I caught him a couple times stealing guilty glances at me, as if he had something on his mind, but he avoided making eye contact. In between my shots on the pool table, I would look over at him, but he'd just turn away and stare deeply into his drink.

As the club's Sgt. at Arms, I was responsible for taking care of the club's problems internally and externally. One of my jobs was to make sure club members followed the club bylaws.

If one member had a problem with another member, they couldn't just handle it on their own. They had to go through me, and I saw to it that the situation was handled properly. I'd have both sides tell me their side of the story, and if I felt one of them had a legitimate beef with the other, they could duke it out behind the clubhouse after the weekly meeting.

If a citizen had a beef with the club, I would handle it, and believe me, I was no ambassador of goodwill. It wasn't good for outsiders to talk shit about us without repercussions. There are two things everyone should know about bikers: we take care of our own, and we love to fight. If we weren't fighting citizens, we were fighting amongst ourselves. But when we weren't fighting, we were partying long and hard.

Lance's body language told me he needed to talk about some shit, but I just wasn't in the mood. I was having a good time and really needed the weekend to relax and have some fun with the guys after what happened last weekend at the Valley of Fire. Riding on this mandatory run to Ash Springs with the club the next day was all I wanted to look forward to — no other bullshit.

I took a long pull from my flask of Jack Daniels and turned my attention back to the felt. My next shot was to sink the nine ball in the corner pocket to take the game. I chalked my tip and sized up my yellow striped target with squinted eyes. I leaned forward and positioned my stick behind the cue ball. I was dead on as I carefully pulled the stick back, ready to claim my kill.

Just as I rammed the stick forward to strike, my peripheral vision caught a glance of Lance, turning again to look at me. I realized too late that my sudden loss of concentration had ruined my shot as the cue ball slammed into the nine, sending them both across the table and into the corner pocket, one behind the other.

I straightened up and threw the stick on the table.

"Sorry about that, Turk," Hiney said, sounding very unremorseful as he held his hand out for payment. "That'll be 10 bucks. Wanna go double or nothing?"

"Hold that thought," I said glaring in Lance's direction. "I've got some business to take care of first."

I was done watching Lance sit there and mope. I huffed over to where he was sipping the dregs of his whiskey coke and smacked him upside the head.

"What the fuck is your problem?" I demanded.

Lance jumped to his feet and squared off as he rubbed the back of his head.

"What the hell was that for?" he shouted.

The bar stood still as everyone waited to see my next move. The only person that had the right to question me was the club president, and he wasn't here now.

"Look asshole, I know you have something to say, so spit it out," I growled.

Suddenly, Lance's eyes darted away from mine. "It's personal, Turk. I'll talk to Baby Huey about it when he gets here."

Lance slid back onto his bar stool and turned his back on me. He picked up his drink and started to take a sip like nothing had happened.

A hot rush of blood flooded my face as I reached around his shoulder and slapped the drink from his fingertips. The highball glass hit him in the chest, and the remaining ice emptied into his lap. Before he could react, I had a handful of his hair and was swinging him around and down off the barstool.

I brought my knee up, and it crashed dead center on his forehead, sending him flying back into a table and some chairs.

Lance laid on the floor for a moment, dazed from the fall. He rolled over onto his knees and pushed himself up to his feet. As his head rose with a ferocious glare, I realized that he hadn't come up empty handed. He had pulled his buck from his boot, and the look on his face told me that he wanted to use it.

I stared at his knife and knew this could end very badly, very quickly. I had confidence in my fighting skills, but the knife put it on a whole new level. This needed to stop before it began.

"That better be Preparation H you're holding, because you know where I'm going to stick that shit when I take it from you."

Evidently, my threat worked, and Lance put his hands up. "Woah, man! Look, I don't want to fight you. Why are you on my ass?"

"You pull a knife on me, and *now* you want to talk?" I shouted. "Fuck you! If you ask me, the talking is over!"

Lance looked around the bar and realized that everyone had stopped and was watching to see his next move. His gaze turned back to me, and for a moment, I thought he was going to lunge at me with the blade. We stared at one another for what seemed like an eternity, neither of us wanting to back down. His head slowly drooped, and his expression turned to one of defeat. He slumped down into a nearby chair and angrily stabbed the knife into the tabletop.

"I can't do this anymore! That's the problem, man. I just can't do this anymore!"

I was struck dumb for a moment before replying, "Let me get this straight — and I hope to hell I'm wrong — but are you saying you want out of the club?"

All the patch holders started yelling obscenities at Lance, and a few tossed their drinks at him.

Some of the members were starting to angrily make their way over to him, and I knew it was going to get ugly, real fast. For a moment, I was content to let the club fulfill their dirty deeds, but at the last minute, I changed my mind.

"Everybody back the hell up! "I shouted. "When it's time to kick his ass, I'll be the one to let you know!"

Stroker, who was standing behind Lance, grabbed him by his shoulders and pulled him up out of the chair, pushing him by the back of the head in my direction. Lance stumbled a few steps forward, then regained his balance and ended up in my face.

"We're waiting!" Stroker yelled.

Stroker hated authority of any kind, including club officers who told him what to do. But honor and dignity among members was what bonded us together, so he backed down in his own defiant way. The group of angry bikers hovering over Lance wanted answers.

"Just let me handle this," I said. I looked at Lance and nodded in the direction of the back door. "Let's go, man."

He turned and headed toward the back of the bar with me right on his tail. Lance had no idea how furious I really was. This shit was fucking up my night, along with my attitude.

Lance shoved the thick metal back door, and it swung open with a loud bang, hitting the wall outside.

We stepped out into the dark and dingy alley that was lit only at our end by a lone, flickering 25-watt bulb. I checked both ends of the dim drive to ensure our privacy. Behind the back fence sat the scrubby, empty rail yard. A lot could happen back here, and no one would ever know.

Lance turned around to face me, and I shoved him hard in the chest, making him stumble backward into the alley. Lance must have suddenly realized how alone he truly was in the abandoned alley, because he started to backpedal and stutter excuses. Everyone knew I took care of the club's dirty business and, for right now, that was him.

"Come on, Turk," he begged. "Tell me you're not going to do what I think you're going to do. Please man, you gotta hear me out!"

"You better talk fast, because I could just do you right now for pulling that blade on me."

He coughed a laugh, incredulous. "I've seen you fight, Turk! You really think I could go up against you without a weapon?" he shook his head, leaning into his defense. "I know you are heavy into that martial arts stuff."

Well, shit — he had a point. "Yeah well, how about explaining to me what you mean by announcing that you can't do this *shit* anymore?" I used air quotes around 'shit' since our 'shit' was the most important thing to our bros. I slowly got into his face. "You haven't been patched for even a year. What's your fucking problem, Lance?"

"Man, I'm just not cut out for this. I didn't realize being with the club was such a full-time gig," he said, staring shame-faced into the dirt. "Shit, Turk. The truth is, this girl I'm seeing now is complaining I don't spend enough time with her. Man, we're just getting going, and we've got problems already!"

"Oh, I get it!" I spat. "You got a new bitch running your life now, and suddenly, your bros aren't good enough for you! Is that it?"

"Man, I knew you wouldn't understand," he said in a small voice. "That's why I wanted to talk to Baby Huey. I just need a little time off to get things straight at home."

"Time off from *us*? We're supposed to be your family, asshole!" I shoved him enough to send him off balance. "Tell me something, Lance. When did you have your balls removed?"

Lance took a step back and held his hands up in submission, thinking I was about to hit him. I saw the weakness in him, and it disgusted me. There was no room for cowards in our ranks. My decision was made.

"I'll make it easy for you," I said in a low voice, contempt dripping from each word. "You have two choices. Either go back inside and wait for Baby Huey, or give me your cut now and end it."

Lance stood stunned for moment, wondering if it really could be that easy to end this.

"What's the catch, Turk?" he asked, his eyes narrowed in suspicion.

"If you go inside and wait for Huey, you'll be on your own. He may be a while, and I think the guys have plans for you. Or you could just hand me your cut and split. I don't ever want to see your punk face around this club again."

"Man, you can't do that! What kind of options are those? You're not taking my patch!"

"I don't think you're in any position to tell me what I can and can't do!" I said, moving towards him. "Guess what? You just ran out of options. Hand me your cut, or I'll take it."

Shit, I thought, *I just gave him another option.*

"There's no talking to you, Turk," he said shaking his head. "I'll take my chances inside."

"Fine then. This oughta be good," I said with a smirk.

I allowed him to push past me. At the door, he turned back and looked at me.

"You act like it's impossible to have friends outside the club."

"Friends? We're your brothers, man. We're all you need. There's something wrong with you if you let a woman control your loyalty. I reward disloyalty with distance. 'Friends' will only fuck you over."

"That's fucked up, Turk. That's not how it is."

"Well, maybe you can't put two and two together, but that's how it adds up to me."

The door slammed shut behind Lance as he entered the lion's den. I squatted against the alley wall by the back door and thought about all the women I'd lost because they couldn't deal with my commitment to the club. But it was a package deal. If they tried to make me choose, I didn't need them in my life. Every time I thought I had met the right girl, she ended up wanting to change me. It just didn't work that way for me. I guess I had become bitter about the whole relationship thing since Tami.

Tami was a great chick when I met her. She had the kind of ocean-blue eyes you could drown in. I had met her at a party and invited her to go for a ride with me on my Harley. She was excited as we pulled out onto the street and roared off.

I knew I rode my bike hard and some would say I was a little crazy, but I was young and that's just how I was. I always pushed myself and my machine to the limits, but Tami didn't seem to mind when I opened up the throttle on the freeway.

On a surface street, I reached back with my left arm and gently rubbed her outer thigh. She took my hand and slowly pushed it back toward the handlebars.

"Please keep both hands on the handlebars at all times," she whispered in my ear.

"What's wrong? You don't like me touching you?" I asked.

"If you're gonna touch me, I want your full attention," she said between the soft kisses she planted on my neck.

I liked her from the moment I saw her and thought that it could turn into something special. After about an hour or so, we returned to the party. I got her number and we started dating. It was nice, and we spent a lot of time together over the next few weeks.

One weekend, we were shooting pool at the Pioneer Saloon in Good Springs when she decided to make her confession. She was in my lap with her arms around my neck, staring at me with those sapphire eyes.

"Turk, I need to tell you something."

"Okay, give it your best shot." I smiled and squeezed her closer to me.

She laid her head down on my shoulder to avoid my gaze and said, "Well, I just might as well blurt it out. I have a girlfriend." After a beat, she added, "Is that going to be a problem?"

I laughed for a moment before I saw her furrowed brow and realized she was serious.

"So what are you telling me?" I asked calmly. "Is your girlfriend jealous of me?"

Her expression softened. "Well ... she doesn't know about you yet," Tami answered, looking away. "The question is, will you be jealous of her?"

"No, baby," I breathed a laugh. "Are you kidding me? I'm not jealous of other women."

"For some reason, I knew you wouldn't mind," she said with a huge grin.

She hugged me tightly, and we made out right there in the bar until someone yelled for us to knock it off and get a room. The fact that she also liked women kind of excited me. I wondered what this could lead to.

Tami's confession had left me wanting to know even more about her. We talked for hours that evening about her life — and about how sad it was when men were involved in it.

When Tami was 13 years old, her uncle had raped her. She didn't talk much to men after that, but when she did finally get married at 18 years old, her husband beat her constantly. After three years of hell with him, she ran away from her home in Montana to Las Vegas.

She was constantly wary of men and exclusively dated women. I was the first man she'd been attracted to in years. I can't tell you how big of an ego boost that was.

We spent the next few months together. I tried hard to treat her right, but her demons never left her, and she couldn't shake her wariness of men — including me. When she found out that I was a black belt and a member of a motorcycle club, it scared the shit out of her.

"Tami," I said gently, as if to a skittish stray, "I've been with you for a long while now, and I've never hurt you. I'm the same."

I felt like I needed to lighten things up a bit, so I changed the subject.

"Hey, Tami?" I asked. "When am I going to meet this girlfriend of yours?"

"I don't know. She may not like you," she said in a deadpan voice.

After a moment, we both burst out laughing.

One of our favorite spots was Mountain Springs Bar. I loved sitting outside on the porch, sipping a cold glass of Jack and taking in the beauty of the tall pine trees. It helped me to relax and ease some tension. The next day, we jumped on the bike and started up the mountain.

The Harley was cruising smoothly at about 70 miles per hour up the steady incline on the two-lane mountain road. A thick forest of Joshua tree catci flew past us in a blur as we sliced our way through the pine-scented air. The early-spring breeze was gorgeous, and so was Tami as she clung to my back and nibbled on my neck. A ways up the mountain, a large black spot appeared up ahead in the middle of the road. I recognized it too late to swerve to avoid it, so we sped right through the massive oil spill.

The bike shook in protest for a couple seconds before it flipped sideways into the air and slammed hard onto the road. In the span of a single moment, my right arm from shoulder to elbow became pinned under the 700-pound machine. My Harley and I slid down the asphalt, and I felt the skin burned and ripped from my flesh.

In the same moment, Tami had been catapulted from the bike and thrown across the pavement like a bloodied rag doll into the desert.

In a split second, the Harley rolled, bringing me with it. It smashed back down onto the pavement, trapping my right leg under the massive, unyielding frame. I was being dragged away at over 70 miles per hour from where Tami lay motionless, with no end in sight.

I could feel the skin on my back being shredded, so I attempted to sit up a bit and balance myself on the wallet in my back pocket. My fingertips were instantly mangled as I pushed my weight from my right shoulder to my butt cheeks. As soon as I was on my ass, I pulled my hands from the road. The metal frame of my bike screamed piercingly as it scraped down the unforgiving blacktop.

I rode down the road on my ass for what seemed like forever until, finally, it began to slow, setting my leg free. The bike let me go, and I rolled in a small circle before coming to a full stop.

I sat up and watched my bike come to a stop in the middle of the road, some 25 feet from me. I gazed down at my feet, taking mental stock of my injuries, making sure that I still had full movement. I glanced down at my right arm but cringed away, a hiss escaping my teeth. That was a little more than I wanted to deal with at the moment.

Suddenly, Tami's voice echoed from a distance. With all the energy I could muster, I strained and got to my feet. My right leg screamed in protest, but I refused to think about right now. I needed to get to Tami. I could hear her yelling my name as I limped towards her. She was about 300 feet away. I couldn't believe that I had slid so far from her and was still able to walk. Tami was kneeling on the side of the road, trying desperately to remove her helmet.

"Tami!" I yelled. "Are you all right?" *Well that was a stupid question*, I thought.

Tami looked up and rose to her feet. She started walking and met me halfway.

"Oh my god!" she cried. "Are you OK?"

"Yeah, baby. I'm fine."

She looked at my arm, her eyes widening like to giant blue saucers.

"No, you're not!" She pointed to my bloodied shoulder.

"Yes, I am," I said, shifting to subtly move my right arm out of view. "Don't worry about me. It's not as bad as it looks."

I was definitely lying — that shit hurt something awful. But standing out in the middle of a desolate, scorching desert wasn't the place to lick your wounds.

"Tami, baby, are you OK?"

Suddenly remembering the smothering helmet, she cried, "No, I'm not! Help me get this damn thing off!"

Her hands were trembling as she tugged fruitlessly against the restraints, so I reached under the helmet and pinched the buckle release. She pulled the half helmet off and tossed it away from her into a scraggly bush. There was a nasty knot forming on the right side of her forehead, already turning a sickening plum color, and her forearms were covered in glistening road rash. Her chin was scuffed up from landing face first on the sandy shoulder, and her tears were turning the grit on her face to streaky clumps of mud.

It felt as if a rock had been dropped in my gut. *It's my fault she's hurt. I promised I'd never hurt her,* I thought before stopping myself. I couldn't think about that now. It was still early, but the July sun was already sitting heavy in the sky, sending heat shimmers along the horizon. As injured as we were, the oppressive heat would only weaken us more, and I could already feel my burnt skin tightening.

"We need to get back to town now," I said as gently as possible.

My Harley lay in the middle of the road like a flattened piece of road kill. *Shit*, I thought. *Why does it have to be so damn far away?* My leg throbbed as if in response to my thoughts of limping over.

I took a step, and my leg buckled slightly. *Come on body, don't give out on me now.*

Tami and I limped back to where my bike was lying. It'd been a bad spill and we both hurt pretty bad, but I kept thinking how lucky we were to even be able to walk at all.

As we limped closer, a car came up the mountain behind us and slowed to a stop near my bike up ahead.

"Are you guys alright?" the driver asked as he climbed out of the sedan.

"We're not sure," I said with total honesty. "Could you help me pick up my bike?"

"Sure," he answered. "You going to try and ride it?" He asked, looking at our injuries with raised eyebrows.

"That's the plan," I said, silently amending, *If she starts, that is.*

The three of us got underneath and hauled her up, pushing her to the side of the road. *Holy shit.* I couldn't believe it. Other than a small ding in the gas tank, a broken mirror, and a few scratches here and there, she was perfectly fine. *Did more damage to us than we did to it,* I thought in disbelief.

I threw my leg over the seat and moved the bent shifter into neutral.

I pushed the starter button, and she roared to life. My entire body relaxed the tension I didn't even know it had been holding.

"I'll be right back. I'm gonna take her for a test ride."

I gave the old girl a little gas and eased out the clutch. She took off down the road like nothing had even happened. She rode well for having rolled and slid on her side for over 300 feet.

I rode up the mountain a short distance, then turned around and headed back for Tami. I pulled up beside her and shut the motor off.

"You guys going to be alright?" asked the driver.

"Yeah, we're good," I said. "Thanks, man. Really glad you stopped." I shook his hand.

"You wouldn't happen to have something to drink, would you?" Tami asked, licking her cracked lips. "I'm really parched."

"No, not really," he answered regretfully. "I have a half a can of soda, but I've been sipping on it. You want it?"

"Oh god, yes please! Anything!" Tami answered excitedly.

The driver reached through his window and handed the tepid soda to Tami.

"If you guys are all right, I'm going to split."

"Sure, man!" I said. "Hey, what's your name?"

"My name's Jim. You? "

"I'm Rick, and this is Tami. Thanks again for your help." I nodded my appreciation.

He nodded back and drove off, leaving us alone on the side of the mountain.

I got back on my bike and started it; she roared with ease. I held my hand out for Tami, but she just shook her head with her lips pressed in a thin, stern line.

"I can't do it," she said. "I can't get back on that thing."

"What are you talking about?" I asked incredulously. "We need to get back to town. It's getting hot, and my arm is burning like shit. Come on!"

"No, I'm not getting back on. I'm walking home." She crossed her arms, staring me down.

"You've got to be kidding me," I said partly to myself. "Let's go! Quit fooling around and get on!"

"No! I'm not going to ride that motorcycle ever again," she said. "Just go ahead without me. I'm walking!"

The shock from the accident was wearing off and was quickly being replaced with pain. I rubbed my temples furiously. This was the last thing I wanted to deal with at the moment, and the pain in my arm and leg was giving me a short fuse.

"Tami … baby …" I said slowly, trying to bring my temper down. "The bike is fine. We need to get home and see a doctor as soon as possible. We're not in great shape right now."

"I know! That's exactly my point!" she shouted, tears beginning to flood her eyes. "Rick, I'm sorry but I can't. That was fucking terrifying, and I won't do it again!"

I looked down at her hands and saw that they were trembling. In fact, her whole body was shaking.

"Look," I said gently, "I'm not leaving you out here alone. It's downhill most of the way. I'll just coast the bike down the mountain next to you. Is that OK?"

"Fine, let's go."

We started down the mountain, Tami walking unsteady, but determined, and me, straddling the bike as it coasted slowly downhill.

After a little ways, I said, "Look, baby, why don't you get on the back of the bike with me and we will coast down the mountain together? I promise, I won't start the engine."

Tami stood thinking for a moment before she walked over and wrapped her arms around me. I flinched when she accidentally rubbed against my burnt arm, but I held her tightly against me anyway. I could feel her tears dampening my shirt as she silently wept.

"OK," she said tentatively, "but just … go as slow as you can."

She climbed on the back and put her arms tightly around my waist. I leaned forward and, after a few steps, the bike was moving on its own again. Twenty minutes later, we were at the bottom of the mountain with about seven miles to go.

"Baby," I said gently, "I need to start the bike now. I'll go slow, I promise."

She didn't say anything, but I felt her shaky nod of approval against my shoulder. When the engine growled to life, it seemed a lot louder than usual. Tami trembled in fear, and I felt her grip around me tighten as I put the bike in gear and eased out the clutch.

I kept her in first gear as we idled at a crawl towards Vegas.

I was just thinking of how it was going to take forever to get home at this rate when she leaned forward and whispered haltingly in my ear, "It's OK. You can go faster. Just — just get me home safe, please."

Oh, thank God. I was entirely sympathetic to Tami's distress, but we needed to get home. I rolled on the throttle and shifted slowly through the gears to fourth. Not only was the sun hard on the raw flesh of my road rash, but now the wind from the speed was starting to irritate it.

When we finally got to my place, I dropped Tami off and headed over to the VA Hospital. A burly, gruff nurse gave me a brutal scrubbing, scraping asphalt and dirt as well as blood and skin remnants from my road rash. That shit hurt almost as bad as the crash itself. She rubbed an antibiotic cream into the wounds on my arm and leg and prescribed some opioids for the pain. I got an extra tube of cream and headed home to treat Tami's wounds.

After hooking Tami up with a rather gentler cleaning than I had received from Nurse Ratched and a good rub-down with the cream, we collapsed into a 12-hour sleep fueled by an adrenaline crash and a couple of pain pills.

A couple days passed but Tami was unable to shake off the crash. She kept reliving it in her mind, repeatedly. She would start crying even at the thought of the accident. I tried to calm her down and help her move past it.

"Tami, we're fine. It's over," I said in a calming tone. "We survived."

"That's not the point, Rick! I thought you were dead," she said, shaking from her sobs.

"What? When did you think that?" I asked incredulously.

"When the bike first went down, and I rolled off the back," she said wiping her nose across her sleeve. "When the bike bounced back up and grabbed your leg, pulling you underneath. You and that bike were rolling so fast, I thought there was no way you could survive that. I was so scared, Rick." Her sapphire eyes glistened as she stared up at me like a lost kitten.

"Hey, it's all right," I said, wiping her face. "We just got a bit skinned up, that's all."

"Rick, it could have been so much worse," she said shaking her head numbly. "Rick … I'm never gonna be able to get back on that bike."

"Sure you will, baby," I said with a weak smile. "You just need to give it a little time."

"No," she said firmly. "I don't even want to think about it. You need to get rid of that bike before it kills you."

"Well, that's not going to happen," I said with a humorless laugh. "It's not the bike's fault we went down. It could have happened to anyone. Besides, it was the bike that got us home off that mountain. I'd say the bike saved our lives."

Tears began to stream down her face again as realization flashed in her eyes. I reached for her to comfort her, but she pulled away, turning her back to me. I think not facing me made what she said after easier.

"You need to choose between me and that bike."

"Tami," I choked. "You can't be serious. I'm not choosing. You just need a little more time." I stroked her back but felt her tense under my hand.

Nothing else was said that night, and we slept back to back. She was gone the next morning, and I haven't seen her since.

The distant cry of a train whistle brought me back to the dank alley in which I was sitting. I looked down at the shadow of road rash on my arm, slowly rubbing my hand across the gnarled skin. Road rash is like a tattoo, but with a better story. It had been almost a year since that accident, but my scarred road rash still took me back to Tami.

Since Tami, it had been hard for me to get close to others. I just felt like I couldn't trust anyone. It got to the point that the only people I trusted were the guys I rode with, so when one of them let me down, I went a little crazy.

Shouts and yells were emanating from the other side of the door and I knew it was on. I smiled into my lap and shook my head. *Poor bastard.* I decided to wait a moment to make sure Lance was totally happy with his choice of them over me.

Above the screams from inside the pub, I heard the loud rumble of a Harley pulling up out front. It had to be Baby Huey and not a minute too soon — they were probably on the brink of killing Lance in there. I stood up and busted through the rear door. I ran past the restrooms and entered the main area of the pub, just in time to see Stroker throw himself on top of Lance. The poor guy was bent over the table face down while Bear and Rotten Ralph held him down. Stroker had his knife out and was advancing menacingly towards the prone figure on the table.

"Stroker!" I yelled above the din. "What the fuck is going on? "

"We had a vote!" Stroker yelled back. "We're taking his patches." He raised the knife for emphasis to a clamor of agreement.

Suddenly, a loud voice thundered through the bar.

"Did you all have a vote without me?" Baby Huey roared.

He was standing in the front door and didn't look at all happy with what he had walked into.

"Put that thing away, Stroker," Huey yelled, "and get the fuck off of him!"

Bear and Rotten Ralph stepped away from the table, but Stroker remained defiant.

When Lance realized his arms were free, he tried to push himself up from the table, but Stroker grabbed him by the back of the hair and rammed his head back down onto the filthy table top. He took his knife and stuck it against the back of Lance's neck.

"Don't you move, asshole," Stroker growled as he looked over at Baby Huey. "If you want this knife, then come and get it."

Two of the biggest animals in our pack were about to go to war, and I didn't want to see the club tear itself apart over a dipshit like Lance.

"Stroker!" I shouted above the commotion. "I agree with you, man, but let's do this together. We don't need to fight over a shithead like Lance. Don't cut off his patch — I want the whole damn vest!"

Stroker paused a moment, then smiled maliciously. He swung the blade up into the air above his head and stabbed it into the tabletop an inch past Lance's face.

"Son of a bitch!" Lance squawked, his eyes widening as he stared at his own reflection in the trembling steel of Stroker's blade.

Stroker grabbed the vest at Lance's shoulder and forcefully yanked it off, jerking Lance's arms back at a harsh angle. He tossed the cut at me, and I snatched it out of the air.

Lance once again tried to push himself from the tabletop, but Stroker kicked the table out from under him, throwing Lance to the floor with a loud crash. The tension was lifted as everyone cheered and laughed.

Lance got to his feet, and I was in front of him before he had a chance to look up. I shoved him back before grabbing him by the collar and tugging his face within inches of my own. I wanted my intentions to come across very clearly.

"If you still want this vest, be at the meeting next Wednesday night. Until then — disappear."

I rolled his cut up and tucked it under my arm. Lance turned and looked to Baby Huey with a waning spark of hope, but he got no reaction from the club president who stared fixedly and stoically past his head. Lance's head sagged as he made his way out the back door, past his gang of disappointed bros.

As soon as the heavy metal door had swung shut, the feeling of normalcy returned to the bar. I looked over and saw Baby Huey and Stroker talking by the entrance, so I made my way over to the bar and ordered three shots of Jack.

The bartender set up the empty shot glasses and splashed the whiskey haphazardly over them.

"They're on the house, Turk," said the bartender gruffly.

"Thanks, man," I said with a nod. "We need these tonight."

I raised two of the shots in the air in Stroker and Huey's direction. They took the hint and headed over.

"So, Lance wants out?" Huey asked, reaching for his shot.

"Guess it's up to him now. I'll keep his cut till next week and let him plead his case in front of the club — if he decides to actually show up, that is." I grabbed my shot and raised it in the air. "We've got better things to think about right now. To our Ash Springs Run tomorrow."

We slammed the shots, slapped each other on the back, and ordered another round.

CHAPTER 3

TRUCK STOP

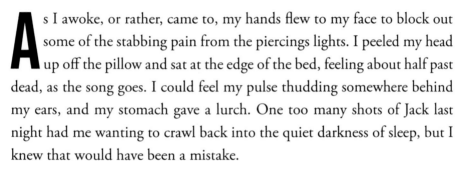

As I awoke, or rather, came to, my hands flew to my face to block out some of the stabbing pain from the piercings lights. I peeled my head up off the pillow and sat at the edge of the bed, feeling about half past dead, as the song goes. I could feel my pulse thudding somewhere behind my ears, and my stomach gave a lurch. One too many shots of Jack last night had me wanting to crawl back into the quiet darkness of sleep, but I knew that would have been a mistake.

It was Saturday morning, and the club was headed to Ash Springs. I threw back the glass of water I had mercifully remembered to pour myself the night before and rose slowly from the bed.

We're not a bunch of early risers, so the meeting time was set for 9 a.m. at the truck stop on Cheyenne. After a quick shower and some breakfast consisting of day-old, cold pizza, I checked my gear and stepped outside. The closer I got to my Harley, the better I felt. I pulled the garage door up and there she was, my 1968 FLH Shovelhead. The morning sunlight cascaded across the chrome on my bike, making her gleam like new. I enjoyed looking at her as much as I loved riding her.

Cecil had repainted my bike after the accident a year ago, and he couldn't believe he was sanding down the fresh paint he had put on her when the bike was his. After the crash, I took advantage of needing some cosmetic work anyway and had Cecil personalize the bike for me. His paintjob was flawless, but it wasn't me. Cecil revamped the bike and made her exactly how I imagined her.

The right tank had a mural of a desert sun rising behind some mountains. A highway curved through the cactus-filled landscape toward the mountains. Flowing out from the left side were ribbons in a rainbow of colors. The rear tail light was molded into the chopped fender with the same tank ribbons outlining it. The whole paint job was done on a glinting cobalt background. The only part that didn't have a personal touch was the front fender — it was just a grey plastic cheapie that I threw on because I had to. I hated front fenders and rode without one as often as possible, but the law was always looking for a reason to pull us over, so it stayed on most of the time.

I threw my leg over, and three kicks later, she roared to life, filling the little garage with her growls. I leaned over toward the workbench and stretched for my skid lid.

I hated those damn things too, so I wore the most unobtrusive half helmet I could find. It had more scratches on it than the inside of a premature burial coffin lid.

I twisted open the throttle and headed north for the rendezvous point. I wasn't more than two blocks from my house when a wasp hit my bare chest and got caught under my vest. Needless to say, neither one of us was happy with the occurrence, but I'm pretty sure I got the short end of the stick.

I tried to pull over to shake the intruder loose, but the damn thing stung me twice before I was able to stop. The first sting caused my right arm to twitch and I nearly lost control of the bike. The second sting just pissed me off as I stepped off the bike and shook my cut, finally setting it free. Wasps are badass and have a temper to match. I plopped down in the grass on the side of the road, staring down at the two angry looking red sores welling up under my rib cage. I hoped this wasn't what my day was going to be like. I shook my head and climbed back onto my Harley with a sigh. *Let's try this again.*

The rising desert sun warmed the skin on my right shoulder as I cruised toward the outskirts of Vegas. I pulled into the truck stop a little after 8:30 and spotted three of my bros at the gas pumps.

I needed to top off since my Harley sported the stock 3 1/2 fat bob tanks. A few members ran the Sportster tanks, which were only 2 1/2 gallons full, but most ran the five-gallon tanks. Stopping for gas was always put into the run plan.

I greeted the guys with a middle finger salute as I pulled up behind their bikes and got three salutes back. I felt a lot of love in the air.

"What's up, Turk?" Baron asked as I stepped off my bike. "I guess we're the early birds."

Baron was a hardcore biker in every sense of the word. He was also the club's alcoholic. He always carried a pint of vodka in his inner vest pocket, but he was ordered by Baby Huey to maintain while riding in formation with the club. If he couldn't manage that, Huey would take his cut.

Baron held his vodka well, and always kept an eye out for Huey when he'd take a sip. That said, I still always made sure I rode in front of Baron. I didn't want him to take me with him if he ever swerved off the road unexpectedly.

"Yeah, well I hate waiting," I said. "So you can bet I won't be early again. What's up with the gas?"

"I gave the cashier $20 to keep pump number 9 on," said Pegleg. "Go ahead and top your bike off, Turk."

"Holy shit — 79 cents a gallon?" I yelled seeing the tag. "You gotta be kidding me! I pay 69 cents over by my house."

"Well, that's a fucking truck stop for you," said Baron with a shrug. "Hell, I remember when it was just a quarter a gallon."

"Well, this is the last time I'll get gas here," I said.

I started to pull the gas hose from the pump but hesitated when I heard the rumble of another Harley pulling up. Looking across the huge lot toward the road, I saw the bike pull in just as a massive semi was pulling out. The trucker slammed on his air brakes, and, with a loud squeal of hard rubber, the truck bounced hard two or three times to a shuddering stop. The biker just flipped the bird to the rig and growled toward where we were standing.

"Who the hell is that?" Baron asked. "Is that Hiney?"

"Yeah, that's him," I said. "That crazy fuck."

Hiney pulled up on his blue and black wishbone rigid-framed Panhead and slid to a stop. The front brake on his 12-inch over Sportster front end was useless. Driving with a suicide clutch was also tricky, but Hiney loved it. He was grinning from ear to ear, and I had to smile back at the lunatic.

Hiney had been my bro from the start. He was the one who brought me into the club, and we've been best friends ever since.

"Did you see that asshole almost hit me?" Hiney asked yanking his helmet off. "That was a fucking close one!"

We stood there shooting the breeze, waiting for everyone else to show up. This was a members-only run, which meant no ol' ladies or friends were invited. We had two or three of these out-of-town runs a year, so we could totally let loose and relax.

I pulled out the pint of Jack Daniels I had tucked away in my inner vest pocket and took a good swig. I passed it over to Hiney and after he took a hit, he handed it to Pegleg who took a short shot and let out a whoop before passing it over to Baron. Baron shook his head and pulled out his stash of vodka.

"What's the problem, Baron? Think I have germs or something?" He said with a laugh.

"I don't drink that rotgut shit. I'm good with my stuff."

"I don't give a shit what you like. You need to do a shot with us for the road, so take this shit," Pegleg said as he pushed the bottle into Baron's chest.

Baron stared at the bottle a moment, before sighing dramatically and raising it to his lips.

"If it will stop you from bitching," Baron said with a smirk.

He tilted the bottle up and started pouring it down his throat. I stepped over and snatched it out of his hands.

"What the fuck, man?" I yelled. "Are you out of your mind?"

"You just figure that out, Turk?"

"You know what, Baron? You need to back the fuck off, and I'm not just talking about being in my face."

I tucked the bottle back into my vest, grabbed the gas handle and started to top off my tanks.

Pegleg was the first to notice the group of truckers approaching us like an angry mob. I still had the gas nozzle in my tank when the truckers, with their fat guts held back by suspenders, started yelling.

"You asshole bikers think you can ride into our truck stop and take it over? Uh-uh. That ain't gonna happen. Which one of you dipshits owns that red bike?" He said, thrusting his meaty finger toward the Harley.

"We all do," yelled Pegleg. "What's it to you?"

"The son-of-a-bitch who rides that red motorcycle almost caused an accident," one trucker said, pausing to spit some brown sludge from between his gums. "You need to get on those damn motorcycles and get your gas elsewhere. We don't want your kind here, so fuck off."

The fat-assed trucker leading the gang of rednecks adjusted his cigar and stood there staring at us as if he owned the place.

"Our kind?" I repeated with a sneer. "And just what kind are we?"

"Biker trash," he said, leaning in and releasing a cloud of smoke into my face. "You're just plain biker trash."

"Really?" I said, squinting against the burning, stale smoke. "What do you think we should do, boys?"

"You know what?" Hiney said. "I think I like it here. I think we're gonna stay a while. Maybe we'll even go inside and have some breakfast."

"Yeah!" Baron laughed. "I want a couple eggs over easy. You taking our orders, fat boy?" Everyone laughed, so Baron added, "Maybe some bacon too", and snorted like a pig.

This really pissed them off — the leader had grown steadily redder as Baron's rant progressed. We were outnumbered, but I had no doubt in my mind that we could stomp these assholes. Still, I wasn't in the mood for an all out brawl, so I decided to solve the problem a little differently.

I removed the gas nozzle from my tank and pointed it at their feet as they moved in on us. With a calm and casual air, I squeezed the handle, and a stream of potent gasoline sprayed the ground in front of them, splashing their boots and pantlegs.

"What the fuck?" shouted one of the truckers amid the chorus of other expletives hurled my direction.

They all stumbled back, almost falling over each other. The look of total shock and disbelief on their faces was priceless.

"Now back the fuck up!" I yelled, breaking my façade of deadly serenity. "The next shot will be aimed at your fucking cigar, dickhead!"

At this, a couple of them flat-ass turned and ran for the café, probably pissing themselves along the way. Two of them just stood there, though, staring us down as if silently trying to call our bluff. Hiney pulled out his Zippo and flicked it open, locking eyes with the remaining truckers. He stepped around his bike toward the pool of gas, only to witness the final two drop their bravado and high-step it away.

Chuckling at their retreat, I finished topping off my tanks and looked over at Baron. He was taking another drink from his bottle of vodka. He looked up at me, smiled, and handed me his bottle. I knew I couldn't refuse after that awesome display of brotherhood, so I took a swig.

"Fuck, Baron," I said wiping my mouth. "That's some pretty smooth shit."

"Smooth as a lady's ass."

"Now, how would you know anything about a lady's ass?"

"Turk, you might be surprised what I wake up with some mornings," Baron said, grinning meaningfully.

"I really don't think I want to know, Baron. Let's put this shit away, we're gonna be riding soon."

These early morning chugs of whiskey and vodka burned in my empty stomach, but that was quickly forgotten as the roar of several Harleys was heard thundering toward us. I stepped out from between the pumps and quickly recognized Baby Huey leading the group as they pulled up to where we were standing.

I walked up to Huey and pointed over to the café where people lined the windows, all staring openly at our ever-growing party.

"We need to hit the road. We had a bit of a beef with the truckers, and they might have called the law."

"Damn it, Turk!" Huey said shaking his head. "Why'd you'd go and fuck this up for us? I want you at my side the rest of this trip so I can keep an eye on you!"

"I know, I know," I said. "Look, take everyone down to Cheyenne and Las Vegas Boulevard to that gas station on the corner. I'll hang out across the street until 9 and grab any late comers, then we'll catch up with you."

"I just told you I didn't want you out of my sight!" barked Huey before he huffed, exasperated. "Shit, just do what you gotta do. So much for a relaxing weekend."

His voice was dripping with disdainful sarcasm, but I was used to it.

Baby Huey slammed his bike into first gear and almost ran me over as he shot past. I wouldn't have expected anything less from him, as annoyed as he was.

I watched everyone leave. As the rumble of their Harleys faded, I was left in somewhat hostile territory. I remembered the look on those truckers' faces when I sprayed the gas at them and smiled.

I looked over at the café windows where the crowd still gawked. I glanced over at the gas pumps and knew I had plenty of ammo in case they decided to come back out. We had only used only about $9 on the pump, so I needed to go back inside for the change.

I walked up to the café and saw everyone that had been at the windows was now scrambling for their seats. I pulled the door open and stepped inside and to the left. Sitting in the corner was a heavy-set, grey-haired lady in a white dress covered in red roses.

"I believe you owe me $11 from pump number 9."

She smiled sweetly, her eyes crinkling into slits, but before she could respond, a voice spoke behind me.

"I got your $11, asshole," the chubby trucker said, as he chewed on the end of his cigar. "What are you going to do about it?"

He had his two buddies behind him for backup, but I had to smile at the three of them. It was like the Three Stooges were trying to intimidate me.

There was a display of cupcakes on the counter. I reached over and grabbed a pack of Twinkies.

"How 'bout this. Let's make a game of it," I said calmly, holding up the treats. "I'm going to try and stuff these Twinkies down your throat. If I can't, you can keep the $11. But if I do make you eat these Twinkies — well, you get to eat some sweets. It's a no-lose situation! C'mon, what do you say? Deal?"

The three of them stared at me as if I were a madman. I think after the gas stunt, they knew I'd really do it.

Suddenly, a meek voice broke the silence.

"Excuse me, sir. I have your $11 right here."

I turned to face the cashier with a gentle smile. "Thank you, ma'am. You're a sweetheart. Would you please be so kind as to take the cost of these Twinkies out of that for me? I think I'll be taking them as a snack for my trip."

She nodded with a timid smile, taken aback by my sudden switch in character back to pleasantly polite.

As an afterthought, just to pick at the truckers a bit more, I added, "You know, if I were you, I wouldn't be smoking with a pant leg soaked in gas."

"Just take your fucking Twinkies and get the hell out of here!" yelled the cigar-smoking trucker.

The cashier nervously rang up the 50 cents and slid the change across the counter to me.

"Keep the change, sweetie. You've been very nice," I said, as I held the Twinkies up for the truckers to see one more time. "Last chance to play, fellas. Whadya say?"

The trucker bit down hard on his cigar and lunged at me, but his friends caught him and held him back.

"Come on, Charlie," his buddy said, straining from the effort of holding the big guy back. "Let him go. It's over."

I stood in the doorway and opened the Twinkies. I pulled one out and ran it under my nose as if I were smelling a fine cigar.

"Damn, you guys don't know what you're missing out on."

I saw Charlie relax as I opened the door and walked out to my bike. It had been a long time since I'd tasted a Twinkie, and it was surprisingly good.

I started my scoot and slowly made my way onto the street. I hooked up with about four more bros who had shown up over the past 10 minutes, and we rode hard to catch up with the rest of the crew. I knew the longer I made Huey wait, the more pissed off he would be.

I led the way into the gas station where I expected to find everyone, but the lot was devoid of Harleys. The five of us stopped our bikes and looked around.

Suddenly, a loud whistle caught our attention. Hawk was waving to us from the bar across the street.

We pulled our bikes across Las Vegas Boulevard and into the bar's parking lot. As we gathered together, Hawk pointed to a set of cop cars sitting down the road on the shoulder.

"They've been eye-balling us since we got here. We're all parked in the back."

I nodded and motioned for everyone to follow me around back.

As we slowly made our way around the corner, I saw all the bikes backed in, lined up neatly in a nice row. Following suit, I shut my motor down and walked over to Hawk, who was holding the back door open for us.

"So what's the big deal about the cops sitting down the road?" I asked, ducking into the merciful shade of the bar. "They've always kept an eye on us."

"Baby Huey seems to think different," Hawk said, shrugging. "I don't know, maybe you should ask him yourself."

"I think I will," I said, a little irritated with Hawk's attitude. "Now go back out front and keep an eye on them. You need to keep us posted."

"Shit, man!" Hawk yelled. "Why can't I come back in and have a beer like everyone else? The cops ain't doing shit down the street!"

"That's not what you were saying a minute ago. Now get your ass back around front!"

Hawk stood there, staring at me with a disgusted look. I stepped up and got in his face, making my intentions very clear.

"If you don't get your ass in gear, I promise you, we will both have to go to the hospital. You to get a boot out of your ass and me to get my boot back."

"Hey man, it's cool," said Hawk holding up his hands in surrender as he turned and headed around front.

I looked around the bar where everyone was drinking their ass off and saw Baby Huey sitting in the back of the pub with a pitcher of beer in his hand.

"That's smart," I said dripping sarcasm as I approached. "Let's get everyone drunk before we go on our 100-mile run to Ash Springs."

"I don't know, Turk," Huey replied dully. "You think getting them thrown in jail is better?"

I started to answer, but Huey slammed the pitched down on the table with a crash.

"Don't say shit, right now, Turk!" Huey fumed, breaking his calm façade. "Hiney tried to take the blame, but when I heard about the stunt you pulled back at the station, it completely over-shadowed Hiney's bad driving."

"Regardless of what happened with the truckers, why are we not on the road? Why did you bring the club in here?"

"Because while we were waiting for you, dumbass, a county cop pulled into the station and was eye-balling us. Within five minutes, three more county boys drove by and stopped across the street. I'm sure you saw them when you pulled in."

"Yeah, I saw them."

"If you ask me, they're waiting to pull us over once we're out in the middle of the desert and bust as many of us as they can for any stupid reason they can come up with!" he yelled. "The run's off!"

"Damn it, Huey!" I yelled back, pounding my fist on the table. "I'm not spending today in a fucking bar."

I was so mad, I couldn't see straight. After what happened in the Valley of Fire last weekend, I didn't want this run to go bad also. I scanned the room, giving everyone a dirty look.

"You know what? Put those damn beers down, now! We're riding today, and that's all there is to it!" I declared.

Baby Huey stood up and kicked his chair, sending it flying halfway across the room. He came at me with murder in his eyes.

"Turk, I've had it with you. You're a dead man!"

"Wait a minute, Huey!" I pleaded.

It wasn't in my character to talk my way out of a fight, but I really wanted to ride and relax today. "Wait just a minute. I've got a plan. Trust me, you'll like this."

At least I hoped he would, but the look on his mug didn't change.

To be honest, I really didn't have a plan B, so I had to come up with something fast.

"I'm not in the mood to listen to a damn thing you have to say. You need to get out of my sight right now."

"The reason you're so mad at me is because you wanted to go on this run as bad as I did. We still can, if you'll just give me a minute," I said calmly. "Just hear me out, and if you don't like my plan, I'll buy you another pitcher of beer, and I'm gone."

Huey stepped up to me. For some reason, if he was going to hit me, I was just going to let it happen. But to my surprise, he wrapped his arm over my shoulder and yanked me in close.

"This better be good," Huey said with a growling sigh. "I'm trying really hard to like you right now, Turk."

He pulled me roughly over to his table, gripping my shoulder a bit harder than the friendly gesture warranted. Everyone gathered around to listen to my plan, and the pressure was on. *That's it,* I thought.

"Look, Ash Springs isn't in the cards this weekend, I know that. But the lake is. We can still head out to the lake on the back roads if we can lose the cops in town. We need to all split out of here by twos, everyone headed in different directions. The club needs to bleed out through the city so the cops have no clue where we are all headed. We'll meet up at Railroad Pass in an hour and ride together to Lake Mead, where we camp out for the night in one of the coves."

"Sounds good so far," Huey said begrudgingly. "Go on."

"We could call Lil' Dave's ol' lady, Chris, to meet us with the chase truck in Boulder City with supplies for the night. What do you think?"

I impressed myself by coming up with a run plan with less than a minute's notice. But all that mattered was if Baby Huey liked it.

"I hate to say it, but that's a damn good plan," said Huey with a grin.

He stood up and with a loud whistle, got everyone's attention.

"All right guys, you heard the man. Start leaving two or three at a time, and don't bunch up. Ride through town a while before heading out to Railroad Pass. We'll meet up with you assholes in an hour."

I stood up, but Huey pushed me back down. He waited until the crowd around us had dissipated before he leaned over the table and got in my face.

"You want to know the truth, Turk? I really loved what you did to those fucking truckers back there. I'm only mad because I didn't think of it first."

He slapped my cheek condescendingly and smacked a big kiss on the top of my head.

"Are you riding with me?" I asked, ignoring the abrupt display of intrepid affection. Huey's always been a bit weird like that.

"No, *you're* riding with *me*," he said, dropping his playful smile slightly. "Let's wait till everyone is gone. We'll head out in a bit. Let's relax here a minute."

I could always tell when something was off about Huey, and the way he told me to hang back was definitely off. "What's on your mind, Huey? Cops got you worried?"

"You know better than that, Turk," Huey answered. "Most of us have our papers in order for the cops, that's not the problem."

"Then what is?"

He looked at me levelly for a moment before sighing. "I don't like talking about it, but if you really want to know, I'll tell you."

"What's up, man?"

"Three months ago, I got pulled over in my car for speeding. When the cops ran my plates, my affiliation with the club popped up."

"So what?" I said automatically alert. "It's not against the law to belong to a club!"

"Yeah, well, they decided to search my car." Huey avoided my gaze and gritted his teeth. "They found my stash of 1000 mini-whites and my revolver."

"Shit, Huey! What did they do?" I asked, openly gaping at his story.

"Well, I didn't have my gun permit on me, so they confiscated my pistol and my stash."

"Did they take you to jail?" I asked, suddenly distracted, reaching back into my memory. "I don't remember you going to jail a few months back."

"That's just it," Huey said. "They gave me a couple citations for speeding and having no gun registration on me and just left."

"What about your mini-whites?"

"That's what I'm trying to tell you," Huey said, finally turning to me. "They didn't say a word about the pills, Turk."

"They busted you red-handed with a shit load of speed and all they did was cite you for an unregistered gun and speeding?"

"That's right," said Huey. "The mini-whites aren't considered a controlled substance, but they took them just the same. But why would they take them, but not take me to jail? Or even write me a citation for it? What kind of bullshit game is that? My court date is Monday, and I'm not sure what to expect. I just want all my shit back."

"Hey man, don't worry," I said slapping him on the back. "If you want, I'll go to court with you, and if anything goes wrong, I'll have the bail money ready."

"Thanks, Turk," said Huey mustering a worried smile. "I'd like that, bro."

"Then it's a done deal. Let's finish these drinks, then go out and give these cops a run for their money."

"I'll drink to that," said Huey, his voice returning to its gruff normal pitch.

I threw back the dregs of my beer and suddenly felt an itch. I pulled my vest back to reveal two red sores almost the size of golf balls. As I rubbed them to relieve the pain, I concluded that fighting with a wasp is not a good start to your day.

CHAPTER 4

RAFFLE

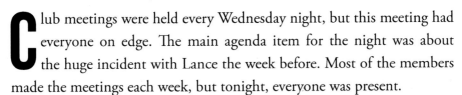

Club meetings were held every Wednesday night, but this meeting had everyone on edge. The main agenda item for the night was about the huge incident with Lance the week before. Most of the members made the meetings each week, but tonight, everyone was present.

Tension filled the air outside the clubhouse as the guys huddled around, everyone expressing opinions about Lance and the scene at the bar five nights ago. Some of them felt that Lance had a right to take a break and try to save his relationship outside the club. Others disagreed proclaiming that if a woman couldn't accept you for what you were, dump her. I knew that family was important, but you don't quit the club to make it right.

I was in the front yard talking to Stroker and Hiney when Baby Huey's figure darkened the front door. He stood there quietly, staring out across the yard in deep thought, not really focusing on anyone. I made my way over to him and waited for him to acknowledge my presence. Huey looked down at me and forced a smile.

"Hey, Turk. I want to thank you again for going to court with me the other day. It made things a whole lot easier to handle."

"Sure, man," I said, waving the small favor away. "No problem. I'm glad you got your gun back, but I'm pissed the judge never brought up your stash of mini-whites."

"I'm betting the cops never even turned them in," Huey said in disgust. "They probably kept them for themselves. Just shows, you can't even trust the cops."

"Yeah well, it's not something you really want to complain about to the judge. The cops knew you wouldn't say anything, which is why they took them and let you off in the first place. But at least all that shit's behind you now," I said, chancing a glance at him from the corner of my eye. "But that's not what's got you wound tight. What else is on your mind? Is it the Lance thing tonight?"

Huey sighed wearily and rubbed his tattooed knuckles. "I have a feeling this is going to be a long night. This club can't agree on anything."

"All we need is a majority vote, one way or the other," I said.

"Come on, Turk! Do you think everyone here will be happy with that? If one side wins, the other side will fight. It's as simple as that."

"Then *we* decide what his fate will be," I said. "If the vote is too split, we'll call it. Then if they want to bitch, it will be with us."

Baby Huey looked past me at everyone in the yard. After a moment, and with a long sigh, he looked back at me.

"Yeah, I guess."

"Have you heard from Lance, yet?" I asked.

"Yeah. Doc went to meet him at Cougars Den," answered Huey. "I didn't want him to ride in alone tonight. Some of these guys are taking this shit personal."

Doc was the club's vice president. He was a tall, heavy-set man with a bald head and a scruffy brown goatee. The man was short on words and big on action.

"Yeah, well, I think everyone should be taking this personally. It's a damn slap in the face and —"

"That's enough, Turk!" Huey cut me off sternly. "You can speak your piece with the rest when the meeting starts."

"Oh, I will. And actually, it's time now," I said checking my watch. "Let's get everyone in the clubhouse, and I'll call Doc to bring Lance in."

"Let's bring the wolves into the den," Huey said with more than a little dissatisfaction in his voice. As he turned to enter the clubhouse, he yelled over his shoulder, "Let's do this!"

The front yard emptied soberly but resolutely into the house. We all knew we had a job to do, even if it was an unpleasant one. The living room filled quickly as each member entered, checking in with me before finding a seat. At each gathering, I was posted at the front door. All firearms were given to me at the start of every meeting for "safekeeping." Rather than protecting the guns, I was protecting the decorum. The meetings always ran much smoother if I had all the weapons. Bikers are infamous for having a quick temper and an itchy trigger-finger.

Baby Huey was lounging at the far end of the living room, calmly observing his very attentive audience. If you didn't know him well, you'd think he was bored by all of this, but I could see the slight rigidity running through his reclined form.

Huey looked up at me and gave me the nod to call Doc. I nodded back and headed to the kitchen to use the wall phone.

"Cougar's Den, John speaking," came a voice on the other end of the line.

"Put Doc on," I said unceremoniously.

"Who's Doc?" John asked.

"He's the big bald dude staring at you right now."

I knew Doc was waiting for a call and figured he would be near the phone to hear it ring.

From a distance, I heard the bartender call out, "Are you Doc?"

I heard a faint affirmation before Doc's voice, now much closer, said "You ready?"

"Yeah, bring him in."

"On our way!"

The line clicked, and I went back to my post at the front door where I leaned against the frame and listened to Baby Huey talk about general club business.

"A couple days back, we tried to ride to Ash Springs, but as you all know, Turk and Hiney screwed that up for us," Huey said to a lightheart-edly jibing ruckus. "Now, I'm not saying we didn't have a great time at the lake, but I still want to ride to Ash Springs. Is everyone with me on this?"

Everyone agreed, so the plans were laid out again for the trip to the hot springs we loved so much. In the middle of Huey finalizing the plans for our run to Ash Springs in a couple weeks, Norton looked around the room and piped up.

"Hey man, ain't Lance supposed to be here?"

Before Huey could answer, I said, "Hey Norton, who put you in charge of taking attendance? You need to shut the fuck up!"

"Damn, Turk. I didn't mean nothing by it. Just, ain't that the main reason we are all here tonight — to deal with Lance?"

"Tell you what, Norton. Why don't you step over here? I need to ex-plain something to you."

I tried to sound as calm as I possibly could, but on the inside, I was ready to explode. I had told the jackass to shut up, and he kept on talking. I hated having to repeat myself.

Norton stood up and picked his way across the crowded floor to where I was standing. Norton stood staring at me dumbly for a moment, waiting for me to talk, but I was done talking. In a flash, I slammed his face into the doorframe with a resounding and sickening crunch and shoved him back. Norton went flying back onto the couch and landed sprawled across the laps of a few members. They yelled obscenities at him and dumped his ass gracelessly onto the floor.

"Anyone else want to interrupt the prez?" I shouted to the mass of onlookers.

The room that was packed to the gills with irrational, hotheaded, and oftentimes-psychotic bikers fell completely still. The silence was out of ut-ter respect for Baby Huey rather than for fear of me. They knew what I represented. They had elected me to keep order, so that's what I did — and

I did it well. If I wasn't good at my post, I'd lose all respect and have to be replaced. So, when I did my job, bitching wasn't allowed.

Norton stood up, cupping his nose with blood gushing through his fingers.

"If you want to take this to the next level, there's always the backyard, Norton. How 'bout it, man?"

"Dat was bullshid, Durk," Norton said inarticulately, trying to suppress the flow of blood that was starting to splash onto the grimy carpet. "You didn'd hab to break my dose."

"I know, but I wanted to make a point," I said with a grin. "And the quickest way to do that is through a man's face."

He glared at me for a moment before pushing his way through the crowd to the bathroom. The brief chorus of laughter that followed the interruption died away quickly as the roar of a couple Harleys signaled that someone had arrived.

A few members stood up and started for the windows to get a better look at who had just pulled up, but I put a quick stop to that.

"Everyone sit down," I shouted. "And stay away from the windows."

"Stroker," Huey yelled from the front, "go out there and make sure that's Doc."

As Stroker walked past me, I jokingly shoved him forward.

"And hurry up," I yelled as he stumbled to the door.

"Fuck you, Turk!" he managed as he turned, a smile cracking.

Trying to ignore our childish horseplay, Huey continued with the meeting's discussion.

"All right, I'm assuming Lance is finally here. No one gets out of line tonight. Is that clear?" Huey said sternly, peering around the room to impress his seriousness.

There was a low murmur of understanding and agreement that was followed by a sudden hush as the front door opened. Doc walked in first, but I threw my arm out, blocking his entrance. I knew he was packing, and I wasn't going to make any exceptions. Doc looked down at my out-stretched hand then brought his glare to eye level. After a brief hesitation and a definite snarl, he reached under his arm into his inner vest pocket and drew out his pistol.

"Don't hurt yourself — it's loaded," Doc said, laying the heavy hunk of metal in my palm. "After all, I know you don't pack."

"No, I don't," I said. "*I* don't need a gun. They just give you a false sense of security. Never carry something that can be taken away and used against you," I added emphatically, hoping he'd remember some of our own tussles that should have taught him that lesson.

"You need to keep working on that karate shit of yours," Doc said, his eyes narrowing. "You never know when you're going to need it." Ah, so he did remember.

"I've always got my hands with me, Doc. What 'bout you? Think you could pull that gun before I slapped the shit out of you?"

"You know what they say, Turk. You can't out run a bullet."

"I've never run from a fight in my life, Doc. Can you say the same?" I knew damn well he could, but it didn't matter.

All pretense of banter dropped from his tone as he pushed into my face. "It's a damn good thing you have my gun, right now."

"Yeah, that's right. Now go sit down before I shoot you in the ass with your own gun."

"Turk!" Baby Huey shouted. "What the hell is the holdup?"

"Nothing!" I yelled back, keeping my stare fixed on Doc.

I waggled Doc's gun in front of his face before stowing it with the others. Doc gave me a middle finger salute, then found his place up front beside Baby Huey.

I could still feel the heft of Doc's pistol in my hand and thought about my Martial Arts training. I started about four years ago as a way to release some pent up aggression and accidentally fell in love with it. What had started out as a stress-reliever became a fixation. Every day I pushed myself harder and harder in the dojo to perfect my fighting skills. I worked out in the dojo three times a week and sparred in a boxing gym every free Saturday I had. Basically, if I wasn't on my bike or at work, I was working out.

I didn't care for guns. They don't give you many options in a confrontation. Besides, to tell you the truth, I didn't trust myself with a gun with my temper and all. But they served a purpose in their own right.

Lance had appeared in the door during my musings and was still standing there, hesitant to jump headfirst into the lion's den. With Doc's gun still in my hand, I glanced over at Lance who was wearing the club vest that Doc had temporarily returned to him at the bar. You had to wear your vest to the club meetings, but tonight we'd decide if he would keep it and stay with the club or if he would leave it behind as he walked out the door.

Lance returned my look with one of barely concealed agitation. His skittishness tickled me, and I couldn't resist. I flashed him a manic smile and raised the gun up to his forehead, pressing the barrel firmly between his brows.

Lance, unsure of how serious I was, stood frozen in the doorway until Stroker appeared behind him to witness our little bubble of faux tension. He rolled his eyes, smiled, and pushed Lance on past me.

"Shit, Turk," Lance said, as he stumbled by me, the color returning to his face. "You trying to be funny or something? What the fuck is the matter with you?"

"I'm never funny, Lance."

I stowed the gun with the others. Stroker stepped up and threw his arm over my shoulders.

"Have I mentioned to you, Turk, that you're a complete asshole?" he laughed.

"Well, Stroker, my momma told me that I could be anything I wanted when I grew up, so I decided to become an asshole."

"Well, you did your mother proud, Turk."

Baby Huey motioned for Lance to stand over to his left.

"Everyone knows about the shit that went down last Friday," said Huey, his arms tightly crossed. "Maybe we were wrong about you. Is there anything you want to say in your defense?"

"There's nothing I could say that can correct the damage that Turk and Stroker have done to my reputation with the club," Lance said throwing daggers with his eyes across the room to where we stood. "All I wanted was time to get my relationship with my girl back on track, but I guess that's too much to ask as far as Turk is concerned."

"And it still is, shithead!" I yelled to a rumble of agreement.

Everyone started yelling various obscenities at Lance as order began to slowly break down. Suddenly, Huey stood up, and silence immediately fell.

"Is that it?" Huey asked with raised eyebrows. "You want a vote now to see if we want you to stay or do you just want out?"

Lance gave a short, humorless laugh. "Those are my only options? In or out? What if I just need a couple months with my girl to see —"

"You think you can just come and go as you please?" Huey roared. He didn't lose his cool often, but when he did, it was a thing to behold. "You think when things get tough, you can just run and hide till it gets better? Why the fuck do you think we're together? This is more than just a club to us, this is our life. If you meet an outsider, they sure as hell better know who you are and what you're a part of before you make plans to build a life with them. Am I making myself clear?"

Throughout his rant, his fiery rage had simmered to a dangerous, low whisper. Somehow, it showed even more fury than his shouts.

"I know, I know, you're right," Lance said, casting pleading glances around the room. It was no use, and he knew it. He had no case.

"Get out of here. The vest belongs to the club!" Huey added as Lance immediately turned to leave. "And what you know about the club stays in that little pee-hole brain of yours. You hear me?"

"I won't say anything, Huey. Come on, man, you know me." Lance shrugged out of his vest, looking at it briefly before Huey snatched it from him and folded it under his arm.

"I thought I did, but I guess not," Huey answered. Lance had the decency to look hurt by this. "I swear Lance, if I hear one thing on the street about you talking about the club, we'll find you. Now get the hell out of my face."

Lance slunk, dejected, through the crowd. He was jostled angrily by his former companions until Stroker stepped menacingly into his path.

"You got off easy tonight, you gutless piece of shit," Stroker breathed as he leaned in, inches from Lance's face. Then he shouted for the rest of the room to hear, "Don't let me catch you drinking at any of our watering holes!"

"Man, this isn't how I wanted things to go down!" Lance shouted, whirling around to look back at Baby Huey. "I don't have a beef with the club — this is my family. I can't ever come back? This is it?"

The sudden roar of angry derision seemed to answer for the majority. But Huey stood silently, his arms still tightly crossed, as his eyes narrowed in consideration.

"Come see me in six months," Huey said when the clamor had died. "We'll *talk* about prospecting you again — if you've got the balls."

I could tell the room wasn't pleased with the thought of leniency, but no one was stupid enough to be as blatantly and directly insubordinate to openly object to Huey's decision. Lance nodded emphatically and made his way over to the front door, where I stood waiting.

"As far as I'm concerned, you've had your chance. You better hope I'm dead before you ever try to come back."

"Who knows, Turk? A lot can happen between now and then."

"A lot can happen right now, if you don't get out of my sight," I growled. Lance ducked silently out into the night, closing the door with a soft click behind him.

Baby Huey smashed the baseball bat he used as a badass gavel down hard on top of the table, bringing everyone back to attention.

Setting the bat-gavel aside, Huey said, "All right, then. Let's get back to the business at hand. The club needs to pad the treasury, so we gotta raise some money. Turk seems to think he has a great plan. Come on up, Turk, and tell us about it."

Our club treasury was fed each month by the members' monthly dues. The money went to supplies for the club runs, gas for the chase truck, and food and drink during outings. Loans from the treasury could also be made out to members for bail and other emergencies. The funds were running low, and we needed a way to fatten the bank. And, since this was Sin City, I had a plan that was unique to this town.

"As Huey said, the treasury is running a little low," I said, clapping my hands together and rubbing them like a greedy villain in a melodrama. "So, my plan is to hold a little raffle to make some easy money."

The whole room buzzed with complaints about having to sell a bunch of raffle tickets to citizens and find something to raffle off.

"Hey, hey! We don't have to come up with anything to raffle off, and the tickets will practically sell themselves. But the best part of this is that we get to party with the winner."

"All right, Turk," said Huey. "You have our attention. Get to the point, wouldya?"

"I call it 'The Piece of Ass Raffle'. The winner gets an all-expense paid trip to Lathrop Wells," I explained, beaming proudly. This was definitely one of my better ideas. "We'll drive the winner up to the cat house, let him pick out a working girl, and party at the bar while she takes good care of him."

Nevada contains the only 12 counties in the U.S. that allow some form of legal prostitution, and Nye County, where Lathop Wells sits 40 miles north of Vegas, is one of them.

"Hey, Turk!" said Spider amid a rumble of approving nods and snickers. "What if a girl wins?"

"Well, I guess I could take care of her," I laughed and swayed my hips, mock-seductively. "Let it be known that I'm not cheap, but I can be had."

Everyone booed and laughed as we discussed the details of the raffle. We decided that the drawing would be held on February 2 at Cecil's Custom Cycle, which was owned by the same Cecil who had sold me my 1968 FLH. The plan was to sell about 500 tickets for a buck each and safely pad the bank.

"Seriously, Turk," Spider repeated. "What if a chick, or even a dude, wins and doesn't want to party with us in Lathop Wells? "

"Well, if they don't want the trip, we'll give them $100 cash instead. Sound good?"

"Works for me," Spider shrugged.

"Look, we have about five months to order the tickets and get them sold before the drawing," I said. "It'll be an easy $400."

"Who are we going to sell these tickets to, though?" Grube piped up.

"They're novelty items," I said, throwing my hands up. "Have you ever heard of a 'Piece of Ass Raffle' before? People will buy them as keepsakes, if nothing else. Besides, it's an easy way for someone to win $100 for just a buck."

Everyone was talking amongst themselves. I had started quite a stir, but the buzz of murmurs sounded generally positive.

"Quiet down, everyone!" yelled Huey, trying to bring order back to the meeting. "According to my calculations, if everyone sells at least 20 tickets, we should meet our goal with no problem. Turk, we'll talk later about the details for the raffle. Right now, I'm ready for a drink!"

I nodded my agreement. "I motion the meeting be adjourned."

"Meeting adjourned!" Huey announced. "Let's get our asses to the Backstreet."

The next two weeks passed slowly until the day of the overdue club run to Ash Springs finally came. I was as excited about this run as I had been about the first one we had planned. I was pissed the beef with the truckers had ruined our trip — Ash Springs is one of my favorite visits.

We really needed to top our tanks off because there was no gas anywhere along the 103-mile stretch of Route 93 between Vegas and Ash Springs. To stroke our egos, or maybe just to twist the knife, our meeting spot was to be at the same truck stop from two weeks ago. Everyone was told to plan their travel time so we'd all arrive together at 9 a.m.

The plan was to just get our gas and leave. We figured the owners of the truck stop would call the cops as soon as they saw us pull up. We didn't want to deal with the law, but we had to show those truckers that we could get our gas wherever we wanted.

I went through my usual ritual of getting ready for a run, but this time I decided to wear a shirt under my vest. Hopefully this time I wouldn't encounter any overly familiar wasps.

CHAPTER 5

ASH SPRINGS

I strolled across the lawn, trudging through the early-morning watering that would be steam in a matter of minutes as the desert sun climbed above Sunrise Mountain. I rolled up the garage door and sighed in delight at the beauty of my pride and joy. The 1968 Harley Shovelhead sat gleaming in the rays of dawn light. She was the perfect bike — a true work of art. The power of the V-twin mill, the impressive speed, and the sleek, alluring paint job. It all resembled what I strived for in the martial arts, the other piece of art in my life.

When I first bought my Harley from Cecil, she was already a flawless beauty, but I made a few minor alterations to truly perfect her. I completely rewired her and installed a hidden kill switch on the frame, just under the seat. I made absolutely sure that this bike wouldn't start unless you hit the kill switch first.

I had installed a Lucas high beam on the frame down tubes just under the triple trees that I'd pulled off a four-wheel drive truck in a junk yard. I knew it packed plenty of candlepower, but I hadn't had a chance to try it out. I couldn't wait to turn it on out on the open road tonight.

I folded my blade and slipped it into my back pocket. I was always prepared for trouble, but today I was really looking forward to it. I wanted payback from those truckers who had screwed up our original run to Ash

Springs. I grabbed my buck from the work bench and stuck it into my boot. Then I tapped my left vest pocket, checking for the ball bearings I always carried. These ball bearings had saved my ass from a crazy cage-driver, and I wasn't going anywhere without them. As the bearings rattled under the pressure of my fingers, I remembered the last time I had to use a set.

It was sometime between late night and early morning as I was leaving the bar. I had drank my share of Jack and just wanted to get home to pass out. The cool night air of early fall filled my lungs as I hit the highway and throttled up to speed.

It was late, and traffic was light, so it seemed like a clear shot all the way home. At least, right up until I pulled behind two cage drivers riding side by side, blocking the highway with their bulky frames. I leaned over, straddling the yellow line, and flashed my high beam, asking politely to pass. For some reason, this irritated the driver, who suddenly slammed his brakes. I had to lock up my tires to keep from rear-ending the bastard. The car then sped up next to the second driver and settled into his same pace, this time purposefully blocking me in.

Since we've already established that I have more than a bit of a temper, it goes without saying that I was more than a little irritated. I just wanted to get my drunk ass home, but now I had to deal with this disrespectful little shit.

I decided to take my chances and kicked her down into third, passing the jerk. I fishtailed a bit in the loose dirt and gravel of the shoulder but managed to bounce ahead of him before slamming her into fourth gear. I was free again with an empty highway ahead of me all the way home. I kicked back in the saddle and relaxed.

It wasn't long, though, before the angry snarl of an engine coming up fast from behind made me sit up and take notice. This wasn't over.

This idiot was now right on my ass. I sped up and tried to pull away from him, but he stayed on my tail. When I changed lanes, he followed in his deadly pursuit, pressing closer and closer. I swear I could almost feel the heat from his engine radiating against the back of my neck.

At this point we had reached about 100 mph, and my heart was pounding as fast as the Shovelhead motor between my legs. *Oh my God. Oh my God. He's going to ram me,* I thought multiple times. Every time he sped closer, I braced for impact before he again retreated ever so slightly.

My mind was reeling as I thought about how easily this guy could kill me and get away. *Wait!* I suddenly remembered what I had tucked away in my vest pocket that morning on a whim. I reached in and pulled out a handful of metal ball bearings.

I checked in my mirrors, but all I could see was his radiator grill. *Fuck you*, I thought, and with a flick of my wrist, I sent a dozen steel balls airborne. They hit his windshield like a shotgun blast. The shriek of tires and smell of burnt rubber filled the air as I watched his headlights veer from side to side across lanes.

"Yeah!" I yelled, adrenaline pounding through my veins. "Hell yeah! Fuck you!"

I pulled over to the right shoulder to have a good look. His car had hopped the median and was stopped in the middle of the freeway, facing north into oncoming traffic. Lucky for him there weren't a lot of cars out that late. I wanted to go back and kick his ass more thoroughly, but I figured I had best get the hell out of there before anyone put two and two together. This little incident had sobered me up, so I twisted the throttle and enjoyed the rest of my ride home.

From that night on, I never left home without my ball bearings, and I feel certain that guy never tailgated another biker.

I patted my vest pocket, smiling faintly at the victorious memory and backed my Harley out into the patch of sunlight cresting over the fence. The mirage of heat haze was already forming over the rises in pavement as I headed out toward the truck stop. It was going to be a scorcher, but the wind whipped my arms, cooling them, as I flew down the highway.

Everyone arrived at the meeting place at 9 a.m. according to plan. We all fueled up without incident. A few of the truck stop regulars came to the windows to stare, searching for signs of a ruckus, but were disappointed by our quiet patronage and slowly began to drift back to the recesses of the cafe. Even some among our own group, myself included, seemed disappointed by the smooth start to the day. But the feeling was soon replaced by a familiar exhilaration as we hit the open road bound for Ash Springs.

About 25 miles out of town, we exited Interstate 15 and took highway 93 North to Alamo. It was a high just being out in the wild air. I was in third position up in front of the pack behind Baby Huey and Doc. On the road, we positioned ourselves according to rank and seniority. I decided to change my position in the group and pulled over into the left lane, slowed down, and let everyone speed past me. I pulled up behind the group, bringing up the rear. We rarely changed positions, but I wanted to enjoy the sight and sound of about 20 bikes ahead of me as we tore through the desert.

The first hour on the road went by way too fast. Before too long, Baby Huey signaled for the group to slow to a stop.

I slowly putted past everyone to the front of the line and pulled up next to Baby Huey. We all climbed off our scoots and stretched.

"What's up?" I asked Huey.

"Gotta empty the tank," Huey answered. "That rigid frame is tough on my bladder."

Several members followed Huey out into the desert to water the cacti. I gazed around, taking in the scenery. There was nothing but arid desert for 60 miles in either direction.

There was something peaceful about being out in the middle of nowhere. It's like for a moment, the world belongs to you. I stepped back over to my bike and straddled the seat facing the rear of my scoot. I leaned back onto the gas tank and folded my hands behind my head like a pillow.

I propped my boots onto the passenger pegs and gazed deeply up at the endless azure sky. A few wisps of clouds looked as if they had been left there by a scraggly, trailing paintbrush. The wind smelled of hot steel and worn asphalt as it blew my hair into my face. I sighed, willing time to stop.

A dull roar mingled with the faraway murmurs of the rest of the guys chatting. I knew that sound. I searched the expanse above and spotted the dot about five miles up. *Aha,* I thought to myself, smiling. I knew I recognized that sound.

The jet sliced through the atmosphere, its bellow enveloping me in memories of my time in the United States Air Force.

I breathed a short laugh. Back then, I tossed my future around like an old sack of laundry. My Dad was the one who made sure I didn't throw it away completely.

When I was 19, the Army sent a notice for me to take my physical down in Richmond, Virginia. I caught the bus at 5 a.m. and spent the day at the base being poked, prodded, and tested. It was another world for me, being yelled at and ordered around by a bunch of loud-mouthed strangers. I always had a problem with authority and never really liked being told what to do — only my Dad had that privilege. When it was all over that afternoon, I gratefully boarded the bus for the 90-mile trip back to Fairfax, Virginia.

Dad was in the kitchen reading the newspaper when I walked in. I didn't know how he'd react to what I'd been up to, so I partially hid myself by opening the fridge door and pretending like I was searching for something during our conversation.

"Where've you been all day?" he asked, thumbing to the next page of his paper.

"Took the bus down to Richmond," I answered, ducking deeper into the refrigerator before adding, "I'm thinking about going into the Army."

I heard the rustle as he set his paper down deliberately on the tabletop. "Really?" he asked without expecting a response. Nevertheless, he paused, and I could feel his stare burrowing through the door of the fridge. "There's no future for you in the Army, son."

"It sure seemed like they had plans for me at the base today," I said a little more confidently, closing the door to the icebox.

"Well, we'll see about that," said Dad. I figured we were in for a knock-down-drag-out, but he only added one thing. "You want a good education, you need to join the Air Force."

Sure enough, the next morning, we headed straight to the recruiter's office. We sat down in front of the desk, and the recruiter just smiled. He offered me the 90-day delayed enlistment plan, and that sounded great to me.

It was a four-year enlistment plan, and I spent my last two years at Nellis Air Force Base, just outside of Las Vegas, Nevada. Being from the Blue Ridge Mountains of Virginia, I was used to a lot of green, but it didn't take long for me to fall in love with the desert. There was something about being able to see for miles and miles to the horizon that made me feel free. In the desert, I never felt caged in. I decided to make Las Vegas my new home and never looked back.

"Turk!" Huey yelled, snapping me back to the present. "Get your lazy ass up, and let's get back on the road."

"Ah, come on, mommy," I said, snuggling mockingly into the saddle like a comfy bed. "Just 10 more minutes."

I was just too comfortable, and the open sky was too hypnotic for me to move just yet. Suddenly, Baby Huey came over and grabbed me by the crotch.

"I've got your mommy, dipshit," he growled. "Now, let's go!"

I shot up, jumping back from him a bit more skittishly than I'd have liked. The chorus of laughter that followed my little prance told me that our embarrassing interaction hadn't gone unnoticed.

"Damn it Huey! That's not funny."

"Neither were you."

Huey grinned devilishly as he threw a leg over his bike. After pumping his starter pedal up a few times, he came up high and came down on the crank with all his weight. The old panhead roared to life, and when Huey looked over at me, we shared a smile.

Every true biker knows the feeling you get when your bike comes alive between your legs. When you rev the engine and you can feel the power flow through the bike and into you — it's like nothing else matters at that moment. All the other bikes were jumping to life — Shovels, Panheads, and even a knucklehead.

After kicking my shovelhead to life, I looked over to see Huey looking at me and pointing at the ground behind him. I knew that's where he wanted me to be — up front with him.

The last half of our trip went much faster. The dry Nevada air had built up a mighty thirst in our throats. As we approached the edges of Alamo, we slowed down. A few people came out to the street to witness our arrival after hearing the low, deep thunder of our motors approaching the dusty small town. Some waved, but most just stood and watched us pass by.

The bar at Ash Springs was another couple miles past Alamo. Some of the guys started getting a little froggy. When they pushed too far past us, Huey waved them down and motioned for them to get back in formation. We didn't want trouble with the Sheriff this early in the game by speeding through the main drag.

Passing through Ash Springs city limits, the hot springs appeared on the right. It looked very inviting with its 20 acres of greenery, but the bar and gas station were on the left, and that's where the guys were headed.

We pulled our bikes into a neat row along the side of the bar. I took a deep stretch, gazing across the highway at the lush trees and bushes of the springs before following the rest of the guys into the cool darkness of the bar.

It was pretty small inside, but it had a pool table in the back, and they served food. The food was all right, but considering we were hungry and it was the only place in town, it was damn near gourmet. Almost everyone went straight for the bar, but a few of us hung back to order some grub. I ordered my burger, fries, and soda and found a table by the jukebox in the corner. Hiney soon joined me. After a few ravenous bites from my burger, I made my way up to the jukebox, still chewing.

As I browsed through the selection, I expected to find a lot of old country music, but instead, I was looking at a large selection of rock and roll from the 1960s. I was impressed and soon had the joint jumping. Of course, I had to play "Born to be Wild" first thing. I made my way back over to my seat and settled in to enjoy the show. As soon as "Get your motor running" hit the air, the guys went crazy, singing and dancing around. *Good to be back, Ash Springs*, I thought as I watched my bros laughing and relaxing.

Several songs later, nothing but a puddle of salty, delicious grease remained on my plate, and it was time to set up camp across the street.

We putted down the dirt road and parked our bikes on the northeast corner of the oasis. Most people parked on the south side of the lot where the water formed a large pond. That part was surrounded by large, shady trees, one of which had a swinging rope hanging over the water. But we always parked a ways away from that area.

We had the back of the lot to ourselves, and that's how we liked it. Bikers don't start trouble if you leave them alone, and we just wanted to do our thing and have a great time this weekend. The townspeople of Ash Springs knew our club. They never refused us a campsite because they knew we always paid the fee they requested for the night's stay. Plus, they knew that as long as we were in town, the bar would make plenty of money, so everyone was happy.

We drank our beer and relaxed in the bathtub-warm, sacred waters the desert offered weary travellers. We had plenty to drink — there was always someone walking over to the bar for a beer run or a friendly game of pool. I could have stayed there forever, soaking in the magical desert oasis, drinking a cold one and laughing with the guys.

Most of us had brought a pair of swim trunks, but others just jumped in with only their underwear on. After a couple hours of beer and hot spring water, though, Baby Huey and Rotten Ralph stripped down as bare as the day they were born. I didn't have a problem with that as long as they kept their distance in the pond.

Late in the evening, as the sun dropped below the mountaintops, bathing the springs in a fiery crimson glow, the last of the guests sloshed out of the springs and wandered toward their car. Baby Huey and Rotten Ralph, still in the buff, decided to walk over to the larger pond with the rope swing. What they didn't know was that the two young ladies that had climbed out of the water, leaving us alone, hadn't actually left the park yet. They were still sitting in their car, checking their maps and preparing to leave.

As the two naked men passed their car, they looked up and screamed bloody murder. They locked their doors and vigorously cranked up their windows as fast as they could, all while shrieking loud enough to wake the dead.

"Oh *shit!*" Huey cried out, trying to cover himself with his hands. "Sorry! We're sorry!" When he realized that they were still incredibly terrified — and still screeching — he walked up to their windows, apologizing the whole way. "We didn't know anyone was here!"

When the rest of us ran up to discover the source of the commotion, all 18 of us half naked, the girls became positively hysterical with fear.

Baby Huey didn't help matters by removing his hands to knock on the window to try to calm them down. Obviously, that wasn't going to happen. Honestly, I really didn't think they heard a word he said over all the screaming. All they saw was a horde of naked men surrounding their car, one of whom was tapping on their window. I yelled at Huey to get away from the car, and some of the others were pushing Rotten Ralph away.

The driver finally managed to get her car started and floored the engine, sending the rear tires spinning as they threw sand and rocks in every direction.

We found ourselves running and ducking to keep from getting hit from flying debris. The car fishtailed through the lot and circled around us. Unable to find the exit through all the dust, the girls almost slid into the pond.

We thought it best to head back to the camp site and let the girls find their own way out to the street. Nothing we did would help their situation, anyway. A couple of us stood out by the bikes and watched as they backed their car up from the pond and made their way out onto the highway.

"What the hell were you thinking?" I yelled at Huey.

"Hey, man," Huey said, staggering about slightly from the beer, sun, and hot springs. "We didn't know anyone was still here. I tried to apologize!"

"Well, I don't think they accepted your apology, Huey."

Huey had the dumbfounded look of a puppy being scolded, and I couldn't help but laugh. Huey stepped forward to give me a hug and brotherly slap on the back, but I jumped back quickly.

"What the fuck are you doing?" I shouted, "I'm not hugging a naked man!"

"Sorry, Turk," Huey apologized, donning his puppy-dog face a little less genuinely this time. "I thought you would enjoy it."

"You're a sick fucker," I answered, shaking my head. "Go put something on before I throw up."

Everyone then started making wise comments about Huey's nudity, and the tension fell away instantly. Soon, we were all laughing, and as we settled back in our campsite the incident with the girls all but faded from memory. As darkness settled over the campsite, a large full moon faintly lit up the springs like a pale lantern.

The stillness of the night was soon broken as two vehicles made their way across the dirt lot towards our campsite. I peered through the trees and could vaguely make out the blue lights of trouble.

"Everyone stay put!" Baby Huey ordered. "Doc, Turk — up here with me."

We walked out in front of the bikes as the town sheriff and a highway patrol unit pulled up to us. Their engines still running, we were blinded by their spotlights. The doors of both vehicles opened simultaneously, and they slowly stepped out as if they had choreographed their movements. With hands on their revolvers, the officers motioned for us to step out in front of their vehicles. Surprisingly, they didn't draw on us — but they sure kept a close eye on our every move.

"Is there a problem, Sheriff?" Huey asked politely.

"We received a call that two girls were attacked by two naked men this evening," the sheriff said gruffly. "You wouldn't know anything about that, would you?" He raised an eyebrow and looked from me to Huey.

"That's terrible, Sheriff! Were they hurt?"

"No, they got away," the sheriff said slowly, narrowing his eyes. "You saying you don't know anything about this?"

"That's right, sir," answered Huey. "We've been partying between here and the bar all day. Must've missed it."

"You're a liar!" yelled the state trooper, a younger fella who seemed much jumpier than the wizened, mustachioed sheriff. "Someone's gonna answer for this — I don't care who!"

The sheriff turned his eyes to the trooper and said gently, "Jim, don't —

"Hey, Chief!" Doc interrupted, his short fuse lit by the gung-ho state trooper. "Why don't you just bring the girls over here to identify the ones that attacked them?"

Judging by the map the girls had pounded against the window to fruitlessly defend themselves from Huey, they weren't from around here. Doc knew those girls were long gone. The two cops shared a look, each hoping the other would have an answer.

"Look," I said, breaking the silence. "We've done nothing wrong here. If you don't have the victims, and you don't have a description of the attackers, you've got nothing."

Years of dealing with the law had taught us a thing or two. I was done playing games and was irritated with the trooper's shitty attitude.

"I need the three of you to put your driver's license and registrations on the hood of my car," the trooper ordered. "Let's see if I have nothing, huh?"

Huey looked at me and rolled his eyes. We stepped over in front of the cruiser, and I could smell the dead bugs cooking on his radiator grill. I found my driver's license and registration in my wallet with the help of the headlights. The trooper grabbed our IDs and called them in, hoping a warrant would pop up. After a few minutes he stepped from the cruiser and threw our cards on the hood of the car with a frustrated scowl.

I smiled sweetly as I picked mine up and stuck it back in my wallet.

"You think this is funny?" the trooper growled.

"Like I said, man. You've got nothing."

"Is that right? I just remembered," replied the trooper, "I need to check the serial numbers on your bike with your registration. Which one is yours, funny man?"

"It's the black and chrome one back there," I said, tossing my head back where all the bikes were parked.

"Wait here," said the trooper.

He strutted past me with his flashlight in hand and headed for the row of bikes. As he was checking all the bikes, looking for mine, I looked at Doc and smiled.

"You know, Turk," said Doc, with a knowing grin, "he's gonna be really pissed off when he realizes that half the bikes parked back there are black and chrome."

"Well, it's not like I lied to him."

A minute later he came back over to us.

"Get over here and point it out!" yelled the cop. "I don't have time for this shit!"

"All you had to do was ask," I simpered, stifling a laugh.

I took him over to my 1968 Harley Shovel, which he reluctantly determined was totally legit. He detained us as long as he could with more stupid questions before finally giving up. The trooper got into his cruiser and peeled out, speeding down the highway. The sheriff stood there alone with us in the dark and just shook his head in the direction of the fading trooper.

"I take it you're in charge of this group," said the sheriff, turning back to look at Baby Huey

"I try to be," said Huey. "You know how that can go sometimes."

"You boys have been here before, never had much trouble," said the sheriff matter-of-factly. "Is that going to change?"

"We like it here, Sheriff. We might get a bit loud and rowdy, but we don't attack women. You have my word on that." Huey gave a firm, respectful nod.

"Well, I think there is more to it than you're telling, but we're done with it for now.

"Are you all leaving in the morning?" the Sheriff asked.

"That's the plan."

"Fine. You guys enjoy the rest of the night. I'll stop by in the morning to see that you all get off OK." He gave a knowing look that said, *And you best be gone by then.*

"Sure thing, Boss!" Huey said. "Thanks for stopping by."

By midnight, we had climbed out of the springs, pruny and relaxed. The bar had just closed for the night, so there wasn't much else to do. Spider fired up a fatty, and everyone passed it around, taking long tokes. The others were joking and coughing, having a good time in their own little circle of the world. I laid on my bed roll, wide awake, and gazed up at the billions of stars that swirled like a glittering oil sheen across the black of the desert sky. The night was as warm as the balmy spring water, and I was getting the itch for a solitary ride.

I got up and rolled up my bedroll before tying it off to the sissy bar on my bike.

"What are you doing, Turk?" Huey's voice came from the darkness.

"Bro, I've had a great day, but I just need to go on a late-night putt," I answered, finishing my last knot. "If I don't come back tonight, don't come looking for me. I may just head on into Vegas."

There was a beat of silence before Huey said, "What's wrong Turk? Did the cops scare ya?"

"Fuck off, Huey," I laughed. "You know that shit doesn't phase me. I'm just not in the mood to camp out tonight, wasting this amazing air, then ride home and roast in the heat of the day tomorrow."

"You need to be here with your bros," Huey said, his tone a bit stiff.

Damn it, I thought. I knew he'd try this. Huey was right, but I just had to get away and being told what to do sure as hell didn't make me want to stay.

"Are you doubting my loyalty to the club?" I asked.

"I'm just saying you need to stay here."

"And I'm telling you I need to leave. You and the guys will do just fine without me." I wasn't going to waste the night arguing with Huey, so I ended the conversation before he could fire back. "Look," I said, slapping him amiably on the shoulder, "call me in the morning when you get back to town. We'll grab some lunch and hang out."

I slapped him on the shoulder and walked back over to my bike, kicking her into action.

The roar from my shorty mufflers sliced through the night air like a shock wave. The calm of the evening was shattered, and everyone jumped up to see what was going on.

I nodded to them and, without saying a word, dropped her into first and throttled my way down the dirt road. In my mirrors I could see Huey's fuming figure slowly receding into the cloud of dust my ride was kicking up. The dirt road soon came to an end, and I was left with a decision. I stared down the dark desert highway, imagining hundreds of shiny eyes staring back. It was the middle of the night with over 100 miles of nothing but open road between me and Las Vegas. *Do I really wanna do this?*

My gas tanks were topped off and the engine purred between my legs. *Yes — this feels right.*

With a twist of the throttle, my Harley came alive and jumped onto the dark highway. As the engine pulled hard through the gears, I gripped the handlebars tighter while the speed tried to pull me from the bike. Within minutes, the Alamo city limits were behind me and a vast plain of no man's land all to myself for the exploring ahead of me.

The ol' shovelhead engine was running strong and kept a steady pace at highway speeds.

The full moon shone for me alone, painting the desert like the deep blue of the ocean. With nothing but open road ahead and no legal speed limits to slow me down, I raced ahead and howled at the moon like the coyotes I sped past.

I looked down at my speedometer and found myself cruising at a comfortable 75 miles an hour. I really wanted this ride to last as long as I could make it, so I dropped the speed down a notch. I found just the right position for my butt on the seat and relaxed my arms.

The suicide throttle acted like a cruise control, and the bike seemed so balanced at this speed that I barely needed to hold onto the bars.

The day spent in the hot springs had completely relaxed my muscles, but the sight of the lane markers flashing under my feet had my heart pounding with the purr of the engine. The road ahead seemed to go on forever, melting into the darkness of the mountains on the horizon. I occasionally throttled my engine up for a few seconds, just to hear my pipes roar. Damn, she sounded good.

A half hour or so into my ride, I started feeling a pain in my bladder. I hated to break my speed, but nature was calling. I slowed down, one gear at a time, letting the motor do all the work instead of the brakes.

A large hill was coming up, where the highway ran through the middle of it. I guess it was easier to cut through a hill, leaving the highway flat than to go over or around it.

I slowed to a stop between the two embankments and shut off the motor. In an instant, there was no sound, no movement, nothing. The wall of silence was a little unnerving at first. A dried stick of sagebrush cracked in the distance, making me jump a bit. I laughed at myself and gazed out over the barren landscape, concentrating to make out any movement. I knew I was alone, but the desert at night is more alive than you may realize.

The curtain of light dropped by the full moon bathed the area in a soft glow. I could see for miles out here. Gazing out over the dusty wasteland, I thought that I could be on the moon right here. I stood still in the silence with only the cracking of the hot pipes on my bike to keep me company.

I turned and scaled the rocky slope. Upon reaching the top, I turned my back from the highway for some form of privacy, and alleviated my urgency. Zipping back up, I looked up and did a 360-degree turn, absorbing my surroundings. The vast desert seemed endless with the mountains rising to meet the starlit sky. Every detail seemed to come in focus, and I saw the desert's real beauty for the first time. It was the middle of the night, and the desert was absorbing me.

A warmth flooded through my body. As I looked over the valley, all my burdens, cares, and worries seemed to slip from my body and into the ground, vanishing completely.

An unfamiliar feeling of peacefulness overcame me. I felt as whole and as calm as I had ever felt in my life. I was a part of the desert as it enveloped me and welcomed me into its untamed calm.

Whether it was some lasting effect of the hot springs or the cool night air pervading my lungs and soul, something was filling me to the brim with quiet, lasting tranquility. I knew in that moment that this night on the hilltop would stay with me until the day I died. I sunk to the ground and crossed my legs, leaning back on my hands and gazing at the night sky as if I were a child first noticing the stars. The spinning of the world seemed to stop as a meteor shower sent streaks of light across the star-studded sky.

I rested there, losing all track of time. I was caught in a trance of shooting stars and wrapped up in the song of the full moon.

I felt that I couldn't move, nor did I want to. My body was no longer mine, but part of a landscape that was a million years old.

My out-of-body moment was soon lost to the lights of a semi-truck cutting through the dark of the desert in the distance. It seemed like an unnatural act, as it disturbed my thoughts and imposed itself on the eternal circadian rhythm of the desert. I reluctantly got to my feet and made my way down the rocky cliff, one step at a time.

By the time I reached my bike, the truck was still a ways off in the distance. I straddled my scoot and paused to gaze once more up at the crest where I had been sitting. It will always be a place of unexplained tranquility for me. I didn't want to leave and resume the loud life I had adopted, but Sin City was calling out to me. I promised myself that I would return to this spot soon.

The roar of my Harley ripped through what remained of the silence when I fired her up. I rumbled back onto the asphalt and started closing the distance between the truck and my speeding bike.

The semi was running his full rack of lamps, so I decided to try out the Lucas lamp I had installed. With a flick of the dash-mounted switch, the road lit up with the candlepower of an aircraft landing-light. I was totally caught off guard by the sudden daylight in front of me.

The trucker obviously didn't appreciate the Lucas light's power, because he started flashing his headlights at me as a signal to drop the candlepower down a notch.

As a road courtesy, I complied, and the floodlight was extinguished. The truck went flying past, air horns blasting, and its back draft slapped me in the face. It was one of the few times I felt a windshield would have served a purpose. I was alone again in the wide, untamed wilderness.

My Harley was a midnight bullet now, speeding over the asphalt with the white lines merging as one beneath me. The cool night air blasted my face causing the tears from my eyes to streak across my cheeks.

There was nothing in sight for miles. I flipped the flood light back on and enjoyed the scenery up ahead. After a couple of miles had rolled under my ass, a little red light appeared on my dash. That wasn't a good sign.

I quickly switched the lamp off and stared at the glowing red light. The high candlepower of the new light must have fried my generator. My bike was running off the juice in my battery, and I didn't know how far that would get me.

Thank God for a full moon, I thought, switching off all my lights.

I needed to conserve my battery power. Driving through the desert by moonlight was riveting, to say the least. I became a speeding shadow in the night with only the sound of my engine giving away my position. It was a thrill ride, as long as my battery held out. Now, if I could just make it to I-15.

My heartbeat slowed a bit when my Harley hit the ramp onto the interstate — at least if I broke down here, someone might find me. The lights of Vegas were in the sky to the south, and my engine seemed to be holding up just fine. Arriving at the Las Vegas city limits, I had to switch my headlight back on.

It had been over an hour and a half after the red light's first appearance when I pulled into my garage. My Harley was still running, and the red light was still glowing.

I counted my blessings to be home safe, but a small part of me was a little disappointed the joyride was over. In a biker's life, there are rides that will be forever embedded in their minds, and that was one of them.

CHAPTER 6

GUARDIAN ANGELS

I t was bound to happen, sooner or later, and it never comes at a good time. I was laid up in bed, dizzy, sore and tired. I had the flu, and it was kicking my ass. I don't care how tough you think you are; when you get sick, all bets are off.

I had been bedridden for two days and was out of food. I was craving chicken noodle soup, so I called my brother, Larry. He told me he would stop by the store and pick up a couple cans for me and bring them over later tonight. It was about four o'clock, so I switched on the TV and waited. I must have dozed off because the next thing I knew, it was after seven and my brother still hadn't showed up.

It was cold and gloomy outside, and it looked like it had just rained. I could hear the cars swishing by my house on the damp pavement.

I sat up and grabbed the glass of tepid water I'd placed on my nightstand the night before and chugged it down. My stomach gurgled for soup, so I made another call. This time there was no answer.

I knew the store was right around the corner from my place, but it was still a little too far to walk in my condition, especially in this weather. I waited another half hour for my brother as my patience slowly waned. He was still a no-show. Now, I was pissed. I wanted that soup, and I wanted it now. I decided to take the bike and get it over with.

I could have called one of my club bros, but I didn't want any of them to ride out in this weather for me and see me in this pitiful, weakened state. Besides, I could hear them now saying shit like, "Oh you poor thing. Are you sick?" or "Do you need a hug to make it feel better?" It was just best they didn't see me like this. After all, I had a reputation to uphold.

I pulled my bike out and scoped out the road condition. I noticed the roads were almost dry in the travel areas from the steady traffic.

I looked up and frowned at the black cloud looming overhead, threatening to burst at any minute. It'd be an easy trip there and back, if I hurried. I had on a thick, heavy coat to keep me extra warm and made my way down the wet street.

The trip there took a matter of minutes, and I even found a spot up by the front door. I shut the motor down and removed my helmet.

Some kid walked up with his groceries and tried his best to irk me. He looked like he was at most 20, but shitheads like these always think they're invincible and go around picking fights trying to prove it.

"Hey, dude," he said, his mocking voice thick on the word 'dude'. "Nice night for a ride, bro."

Typically I'd have knocked the punk back easily, but I was in no mood for this, so I kept my mouth shut. I stepped away from my bike and checked his shoulder hard as I walked past him.

"Hey man," he said, all sarcasm dropping. "Watch it, you meathead!"

I stopped at the door and hesitated a moment, but took a deep breath and walked inside. *Not tonight. I just don't feel like doing this tonight.* I grabbed four cans of soup and was through the checkout line and back on my bike in no time.

My coat pockets were large enough to carry two cans each, so instead of trying to ride home while fumbling with a paper bag, I slipped the cans inside. I idled through the parking lot to Decatur Boulevard and waited for a break in traffic to make my left turn. There seemed to be an endless stream of cars for this time of night, and I was getting impatient. I was beginning to feel a woozy weakness coming on, and I just wanted to get home as fast as I could.

I noticed a small break in the line of cars and I took it. I gunned my motor, flinging a spray of water in my wake, and squeezed into traffic.

I know for a fact that I hadn't cut off the guy behind me as I found my hole in the line of cars, but he laid on his horn and drove up my ass just the same.

I made a left onto Twain and he followed, not giving me much room to even breathe. *Why now? why tonight? I just want to go home and enjoy my soup*, I thought. I pulled my Harley to the side of the road and waited for him to pass. But instead, he pulled around in front of me on the side and came to a stop.

I found myself staring at the tail lights of a 1964 Chevy Impala, a favorite model of mine. I stayed on my bike as the driver's door swung open and the same young shithead from the grocery store stepped out. *God dammit*, I thought, cursing the universe's sick sense of humor. The dude stared at me for a brief moment, recognized me, then reached down into the rear floorboard of his car before coming back up with a baseball bat.

For a split second, I thought about just speeding off, but my damn Irish pride wouldn't let me. I don't turn and run from anything. I rose from my bike and took off my jacket, sighing in resignation. I held my jacket by its collar and felt the weight of the soup cans in its pockets, smiling faintly to myself. The young punk waited only a beat before rushing me, the bat cocked over his right shoulder, ready to be swung when he came within range.

I faked like I was going to charge at him and he swung, missing me by a mile. I faked an attack at him again, and he also missed again. While it was fun to mess with him, I was also timing his swings. Just like so many others, this guy was nothing but an ego with a weapon he didn't know how to properly use in a real fight. On the third swing, I made my move.

As the bat came around, I swung my jacket with all the energy I had left at that moment, and the soup cans made contact with the left side of his head. I turned my back into his right shoulder and smothered the speed of the on-coming bat. I released my jacket, letting the cans clatter over to the curb, and grabbed his right arm, pulling him over my shoulder with a judo throw. He landed on his back in front of me, the air rushing out of his lungs in a heavy *humph!* as the bat rolled from his hand to the edge of the street.

I dropped my knee into his chest and wrapped my hands around his throat. He grabbed my wrists and pulled hard in an attempt to break the choke hold I had on him. He was right where I wanted him.

I knew this had to end soon because my strength was draining fast. A cold sweat had begun to break out during the fight as my fever rose with the exertion. Thank God the soup cans had dazed him, because as weak as I was getting, this might not have ended well. My mind was racing to figure out my next move.

I wasn't about to murder the kid over a case of road rage and poor judgment, so I figured I'd let him up and see what he had left.

Just as I loosened my grip on his windpipe, something hard hit me in the kidney. I looked down at the purple kid I was choking to see his hands still wrapped feebly around my wrists. *What the fuck just hit me, then?* Suddenly, I was hit square in the nape of the neck by something cold and rough.

I sprang to my feet and whirled around, searching for a new assailant. There had been two passengers in the car, I guess. The other asshole had gotten out and bravely decided to just throw rocks at me from the side of the road. *You have got to be kidding me,* I thought.

I started after him, but the coward bolted after I had taken a few steps, stopping only long enough to sling one final rock at me. This time, the idiot didn't aim very well, and the rock hit their own car with a loud bang, shattering the passenger window.

I turned back to the driver and saw that he had gotten to his feet and was gingerly rubbing the side of his head.

"What the fuck did you hit me with?" he asked, looking down at my jacket at his feet.

"My dinner," I answered. "Come on, asshole. Let's finish this."

He breathed a quick, humorless laugh. "Fuck you, man!" he said, bolting to his car.

He slammed the door firmly behind him, sending pieces of glass from the other window tinkling down to the pavement. The tires broke loose on the wet asphalt and spun wildly down the street. The car picked up speed as he gained traction on the dry area of the road, and the young shithead disappeared into the night, his thirst for trouble likely slaked for a good while.

I was so glad it was over; I could hardly stand. I walked back toward my bike and stopped to pick up my jacket. I saw the bat lying on the side of the road and decided to keep it as a souvenir. With a slight groan, I pulled my bike up off the kickstand — even that much effort killed me. Sitting there a moment as the Harley vibrated between my legs gave me time to collect my thoughts.

I took a couple of deep breaths, balanced the bat on the handlebars in each hand, and pushed the shifter into first gear with a loud clunk. I putted the rest of the way home, trying not to pass out from exhaustion along the way.

I finally pulled into my garage, shut off the bike, and laid on the gas tank a minute or two to relax. The warmth from the engine felt good against my clammy skin. Time slipped by and I passed out on the bike, lulled to sleep by the stillness of the garage. A violent, cold shiver woke me. I pulled my coat up around my neck, shaking from head to toe. I was freezing on the outside and burning up on the inside.

What the hell happened? All I wanted to do was get a couple cans of soup. *My soup!* I quickly tapped the sides of my jacket and my heart slowed again as I felt all four cans in place. I must have slipped them back into my pockets after collecting my souvenir bat. The garage was getting colder, so I forced myself out of the saddle and into the house.

I threw two cans of soup into a pan and stared dazedly at the murky liquid until it boiled. I gotta tell you, that chicken noodle soup sat warm and soothingly in my belly, and I slept like a baby for the next 12 hours.

By the next evening, I was starting to feel much better. I gave my brother a call to give him shit for making his poor, ill brother fend for himself.

"Ricardo? Oh shit, man! Hearing your voice just reminded me you wanted me to grab some soup for you. I'm so sorry, man. I totally spaced it out," he frantically apologized.

"You have no idea what you put me through. That was a damn struggle."

"Look, I'm on my way to the Inn Zone for dinner. How about I buy you a drink and dinner to make it up to you?"

"OK, sounds good, but I'm having the steak," I said. "I've got cabin fever and a story to tell you. You gotta pick me up, though. I don't feel like riding tonight."

"Cool, I'll be there in about 20 minutes."

My brother Larry was a Born Again Christian, but he still loved his beer. He had a strong heart for family and Jesus, but his body was weak for alcohol. Don't get me wrong — I'm definitely not one to preach on how someone should lead his life, because I'm far from perfect. We all have our demons to deal with, and believe me, I have mine. He was my brother, and I accepted him for who he was.

When we sat down at the bar, I ordered my regular, a Jack and Coke, and he ordered one, too. I didn't usually approve of him drinking hard alcohol, but that night I thought, what the hell? We saw the bottom of that bottle of Jack and polished off a couple of rib eyes. It was almost time to pick up and leave when Larry looked over my shoulder. He turned back to his drink and gave a pissed off sigh.

"I thought you had my back, man," he muttered sulkily.

"What?" I asked, taken aback. "What the hell are you talking about?" I was in disbelief that he would say something like that. Larry and I have always been there for each other, no matter what.

"Those people behind us …" he trailed off, still staring into his drink, avoiding my eyes.

I looked behind me and no one was there. "What are you talking about, Larry? There's no one behind us."

He looked behind us again, then quickly changed his expression and turned back around to his drink.

"Never mind," he said.

"Don't 'never mind' me. You just opened a can of worms saying I didn't have your back. What the hell are you talking about?"

He opened his mouth, but closed it and shook his head. "You wouldn't believe me if I told you," he said. "Just forget it."

"Are you kidding me? No, I'm not forgetting it!" I said, getting frustrated. "What did you mean?"

"Alright," he sighed. "I know you're not going to believe this but … you have three guardian angels standing behind you."

I checked over my shoulder one more time, honestly half-expecting to see three white-clad figures; his voice was just so sincere. There was still nothing there. I internally shook off my moment of credence. *He's had a bit much*, I thought looking at my brother's imploring eyes. I decided not to argue.

"Is that good?" I asked gently, smiling encouragingly.

"Yeah, that's real good!" Larry's face lit up in excitement at my acquiescent response.

"Well, that's nice to know." I threw back the rest of my drink and rose to my feet, clapping him on the back. "Now let's get out of here before all that Jack you chugged screws with your driving. I hope you don't need my guardian angels to get us home safe!"

"Dammit, Ricardo!" he said, throwing off my arm. "I knew you wouldn't take me seriously."

"Hey, I believe you, man. It's nice to know, really!" I wondered to myself if he'd had enough Jack that he'd be able to see through my very thin façade.

I had never been told that I had guardian angels before, so I didn't really know what else to say. Larry seemed to suspect my sincerity, but the moment passed as we paid our tab and headed out to the car.

Larry and I were headed back toward my place when it caught my eye. I spun around in my seat and stared out through the dew-dropped rear window.

"Larry, turn around — quick!"

"Come on, Ricardo, I just want to go home," Larry mumbled.

"I'm not kidding! Turn the damn car around!"

He looked over at me, his annoyance plain, but he slammed on the brakes and whipped the car around nonetheless. We headed back the way we'd come, and there she was. I couldn't believe my eyes.

"Stop, stop, stop!" I shouted, leaning forward excitedly. There beside us was the 1964 Chevy Impala from the night before, broken down on the side of the road like a gift from above.

"Larry, that's the car that belonged to the assholes who jumped me last night with a baseball bat!"

I jumped out of the car before Larry had a chance to respond. I had to be sure this was the same car. I walked up on the right side to find bits of shattered glass still clinging to the window frame on the passenger side from a hastily thrown rock. That's all I needed to see. How in the hell did I get so lucky?

I walked back to where Larry was sitting in the car, waiting with a confused expression.

"Give me the keys to the trunk," I said.

"What are you going to do?" he asked, handing me the keys.

I gave a mischievous grin and a waggled of the eyebrows before walking back behind the car. After a quick scan around the area to see if anyone was watching, I popped the trunk and grabbed the tire iron.

"Pull the car across the street to that gas station," I said, tossing the car keys into Larry's lap through the open window. "I'll be there in just a second."

With a resigned click of the teeth and a roll of the eyes, Larry made a U-turn into the station. I looked around to see if any cars were coming as I walked to the front of the car. After another quick glance around, I bashed his headlights in with four quick swings. And just for good measure, I also left a respectable dent on the hood.

I would much rather it had been his head, but I guess you can call me a softy. It hurt to leave that final dent on such a gorgeous car, but I was drunk, and it seemed like a good way to get even at the time.

I ran across the street and climbed into my brother's car, my vengeful adrenaline still pumping.

"Man, I feel *much* better now!" I said with a resounding *whoop!*

That feeling didn't last long, though, because after getting home, I couldn't stop thinking about that shithead. Even after beating his car to shit, I still felt like I had unsettled business.

I jumped on my bike and rode back down to the abandoned Chevy. I didn't know why I was going back — what else was there left to do to that poor car? I felt like an arsonist returning to view the ashy ruin of a building he'd razed as I pulled up behind the Impala.

What am I doing here? I thought to myself. I chewed the inside of my cheek as I inspected the car. My eyes fell on the license plate, and a wicked grin broke out across my face. That's all I needed.

The next day I passed the license number to a friend's wife who worked for the police department. In less than an hour, I had a name and an address.

Sitting in the parking lot of the police department, I looked at the information scratched into my notebook and smiled. I wanted to savor the hunt, so I decided to wait until Friday night to pay him a visit.

A few days later, I pulled up across the street from the ramshackle house. The bashed up Impala was sitting out front in the street while a second car occupied the driveway. I checked the headlights on the '64 Chevy, saw that only the two driving lights had been replaced, and allowed myself a petty little grin.

I leaned against my bike, not sure of what my plan was. I had brought his baseball bat with me and was going to make sure he got it back one way or another. I sat there reliving the events of that night and how sick I was. Nobody enjoys having to fend off some asshole trying to bash in their head, but especially not when you've got the flu. And the rocks! His little bitch of a friend threw rocks at me instead of actually joining the fight! At least the first shithead had the balls to face me. Now that I had my strength back, we'd see how tough he is.

I wasn't about to knock down the door and slug him, but I'd sure as shit wait here until he reared his ugly head and I could face him in the street. After about an hour of twiddling my thumbs and watching the grass grow, I was about ready to call it quits when the front door opened. He didn't notice me as he trudged through his yard to his car.

As he pushed his key into the door lock, I fired up my Harley. The sound of my pipes tore through the silent night air like a freight train.

It must have truly scared the shit out of him, because he swung around and braced himself on the door of his car, quaking in his boots.

With the baseball bat perched carefully across my lap, I full-throttled my Harley across the street at him and stopped just short of running his ass over. My front tire was between his legs, mere inches from the jewels. The guy was pinned to his car, his hands feebly holding onto my handlebars as he shook in place, too scared to move.

I took the bat, cocked my head slowly, and gave one, quick rap of the bat against my open palm.

"You want to try this again?" I asked calmly, raising my brows.

"Wh— Who are you?" he stuttered. "What the hell do you want?"

I tossed the bat at his feet and tilted the bike over onto its kickstand.

"Come on, dude!" I said raising my hands disbelievingly. "Don't you remember where you left your bat?"

He peeled his saucer-wide eyes from mine and looked down at the bat before looking back up with a face of sheer panic. I stepped off my scoot and looked at him appraisingly for a moment before suddenly pushing myself up into his face.

"Come on tough guy. Let's get started," I whispered against his cheek, which was wet, either from sweat or tears.

The kid glanced over his shoulder at the house, obviously hoping someone might have spotted the situation through a window and would come save his ass, but there was no movement from the house. When he looked back at me, he came face to face with my knife pressed blade-down against his blackhead-strewn nose.

The punk didn't even have time to piss himself before I'd grabbed a handful of hair and pushed his head back, exposing a patchy-bearded neck.

"What's wrong, man?" I asked, rubbing the knife blade back and forth across his throat. "Don't wanna play anymore? You sure wanted to play the other night when you tried to take my head off with this fucking bat!"

"Come on, man!" he sobbed. "I'm sorry, dude. What do you want from me?" His voice cracked at the end of the tearful plea, and I realized that this kid probably *wasn't* older than 20 like I'd estimated the other night.

"How old are you?" I asked.

"Why the fuck do you care?" he shouted, sending bits of spit flinging.

I pressed the flat of the blade a bit more firmly into the pimply skin of his neck.

"You seriously wanna talk like that to me right now? Does that really seem like a great idea?" I asked incredulously. "Your life doesn't mean a damn thing to me, so I'll ask again, and I'd suggest you answer. How old are you, fucker?"

"18! I'm 18!" his voice cracked again.

"Son of a bitch," I mumbled. I sighed and stepped back, slipping my knife back in its sheath.

"You're just some fucking punk kid whose balls haven't dropped," I said gruffly.

Kids that age are so fucking stupid, going around picking fights to prove their manhood. Shithead shouldn't have been so stupid as to go around picking fights with random bikers, but I definitely remembered a few stupid things I'd done at that age.

Still, I thought, *the little prick should walk away with a bit more than some piss-soaked pants to teach him a lesson.*

I stooped down and picked up the baseball bat. "You want your bat back?" I asked, holding it out.

"I-it's OK. You keep it!"

"I don't want it," I said. "Here, I'll put it back in the car for you."

I raised the bat and gave it my best Mickey Mantle swing towards the kid's head. He dodged as I expected he would, dropping to his knees as the bat smashed into the driver's side window with a loud crash. Glass flew all over the kid's head as the bat dangled from the shattered window. I figured two smashed windows and a pair of ruined pants would serve as a memorable lesson.

"Guess it's your lucky day, kid," I said as I clapped my hands together. "But a word to the wise — I'd think twice before starting another fight with a biker. He might not be as nice as me."

With one final grin, I threw my leg over my bike and kicked life back into it. I backed her away slowly to make a U-turn before heading home but wanted one last shot of fun. I idled for a moment, and as the kid raised his head, I screeched toward him, sending him high-tailing back across the yard to his house.

I laughed the whole way home.

I hadn't thought about my conversation with Larry at the Inn Zone until one night, weeks later, at a local pub when a guy sauntered in, laughing his ass off and hanging onto some chick.

They sat a few stools away from where I was sitting with some of my bros, and my curiosity got the best of me.

"What's so funny?" I asked.

"Well, I just met this lady outside in the parking lot, and she told me she was a psychic," he said clapping the woman on the shoulder. "She's been telling me stuff about my life that there's no way she could know."

"Is that so?" I asked, turning my patronizing smile to his lady friend. "Do you read minds?"

"No, I don't read minds," she said, flashing a set of straight, white teeth. "I can just see things in people."

"Huh, well that's cool," I said. "You guys have fun."

I didn't believe in that mojo stuff. I went back to my conversation with my bros, but I could still feel the woman's steely grey eyes on my back.

After a few minutes, I got up from my seat and headed for the bathroom. As I walked past the guy and his lady friend, she reached out and grabbed ahold of my sleeve.

"Hey, fella," she said kindly. "Sorry — I didn't catch your name."

"My friends call me Turk. What about you?"

"I've been called a lot of things, but I think I like Misti the best."

"Well, Misti, it's nice to meet you."

She gazed at me a moment before saying, "Did you know you have three guardian angels behind you, Turk?"

A chill ran through my spine, and my talk with Larry flashed in my mind. I smiled but said nothing, then turned and walked into the bathroom.

I looked at myself in the mirror for a long time. I didn't really know what I was looking for behind me, but I stared just the same. I didn't believe in angels, but shit, I was thinking I might have to start. A couple angels might certainly help explain how I survived some of the rougher and stupider shit I've found myself a part of in the past.

The first time my angels had been mentioned, I didn't think twice about it; the second time, I was covered in gooseflesh; but by the time it happened again, I had almost expected to hear more about the angels. It actually happened again while my buddies and I were out drinking at another local pub. The gorgeous Jamaican cook was walking around behind the bar, so I asked her to take a picture of the guys and me. She obliged, and we all gathered together with our arms wrapped around one another, waiting for the flash. She paused a moment and looked over the camera at me.

"Hey, man," she said in a thick accent with eyes as wide as manhole covers. "You know you got three guardian angels behind you?"

"I know, I know. Just take the picture."

At this point I'd just accepted my permanent companions. I just hoped I didn't do something to piss them off.

CHAPTER 7

ERNIE'S PLACE

The following weekend, I found myself hiking up the steep side of a cliff at Mount Charleston with some of the bros. Our steel-toed engineer boots were not the ideal wear for this trek, but we were having fun on this unplanned expedition in the mountains. Our bikes were parked beside the road about halfway down the mountain, near the lodge. Just for shits and grins, we decided to hike up through the dense trees, just for something to do.

I was leading the way up and was way ahead of the others. Having grown up in the Blue Ridge Mountains of Virginia, I was accustomed to tramping through thick woods, but the rest of the guys weren't. I stopped to rest and wait for my bros to catch up at an overhang that overlooked a gorge. Having lived in the Las Vegas desert for the past five years made me really appreciate these trips to Mount Charleston.

I settled in on a fallen tree trunk and waited for Stroker, Hiney, and Pegleg to catch up. I laid back and took in the beauty of the trees stretching to graze the azure sky. A cool mountain breeze whispered through the treetops, and the clean mountain air transported me back to my days of growing up on the farm in Virginia. I felt very fortunate that I had grown from a boy to a man in the foothills of the Appalachians rather than some big city. Life was so much simpler back then.

Mountain folk and city folk are different — back then we grew our own food. We were poor, but we didn't realize it. We didn't have welfare or food stamps, but we made do with what we had. Everyone was family back then, and families hunted together, farmed together, and stuck together. My dad once told me, "When the roots are deep, there is no reason to fear the wind." That's why I loved the club — we were family.

When I was a kid back in the early '60s, you had to be imaginative and inventive. The nearest store was in a town about 30 miles away called Lexington, and on Christmas and birthdays, you usually got clothes. If you wanted toys, you had to make them from the stuff lying around on the farm.

Which is why, when I was about 14 years old, I decided to build my own motorcycle. My grandfather had given me this old two-stroke riding lawn mower, and I had visions of taking that engine and turning my bicycle into a motorcycle.

I stuck a wooden spool over the horizontal shaft of the engine and set the motor in the frame so that the spool would roll against the rear tire. The engine was bolted onto a piece of plywood and secured to the frame with a couple u-clamps and some bailing wire. I'd hold the throttle wire in my left hand and steer with my right.

After a day of playing around with the engine, and with help from my dad and grandfather, a few good pulls on the starter rope finally brought her to life. I was so proud watching the motor idle in my bicycle frame. I knew in that moment that something in my life had changed.

I stretched my leg over the bike and could feel the engine vibrate through every bone in my body. The makeshift motorcycle was roaring and shaking it's way into becoming a part of me.

I couldn't wait any longer. With a face-splitting grin, I pulled the throttle wire and was off and running. I faintly heard my dad yell, "Be careful, son!" as I bounced down the dirt road away from him. I couldn't believe it — I was riding a motorcycle I'd crafted with my own two hands.

I yanked the wire and gave it more gas. I was tearing down that old dirt road, dodging rocks and potholes and gaining more and more speed.

I should have made the throttle cable at least two inches longer because I could only reach my handlebar with my left hand if I was at full throttle. I made a mental note to correct that when I got back to the barn. But at the moment, I was at full throttle, both hands on the handlebars, and I wasn't slowing down for anything.

The crisp mountain air lashed my cheeks as I tore down the dirt road, feeling more alive than I'd ever felt before. It would have been the most perfect, unmarred moment in life if I'd tested the brakes a bit more thoroughly or if it weren't for those damn cows.

I veered around a bend in the road and came face to face with five half-ton roadblocks in the form of my grandfather's dairy cows. The beasts were blocking the entire lane. I tried to slow down, but my rear brakes didn't seem to work with the spool spinning against the rear tire. I was picturing myself plowing into the side of a massive cow when I noticed that the sound of my engine was beginning to scare them as I got closer. They scattered as fast as their hulking figures would allow and ran up the hill to escape the monster they thought I was.

I was within 50 feet of the fatal wall of bovine when a spot just wide enough to squeeze through opened up before me. I let out a rebel yell and gunned it. I pushed her as fast as she would go, the road bouncing me up and down like I was on a bronco. I was having the time of my life and didn't want this adventure to end.

I didn't take into consideration that the rear tire might not have been able to handle the speed or the heat from the spinning spool. Suddenly, there was a loud *bang* from the rear tire as the bike jerked to the right, sending me, and the bike, over a four-foot embankment. I flew through the air for what seemed like an eternity before landing on my ass in the creek.

I shot up from the icy water and covered my head as the bike crashed just a few yards in front of me. The steam rose with a hissing sound from the engine as it sank into the shallow creek at my feet. The busted frame of my bike had separated completely from the engine and had floated downstream a short distance from where I sat.

I stood up in the rock-laden, muddy water and checked myself for broken limbs. My ass was sore, and my elbows and knees were scratched up, but other than that, I was fine. I watched as the current carried my engine a few feet past me before lodging it between two rocks. The frame lay broken halfway on the bank, exposing a bent front rim and busted spokes. I decided to leave it in its watery grave and walked the mile or so back to the farmhouse, sopping and sulking.

It took me a week to build my first motorbike and less than an hour to destroy it. I was only 14 years old but could feel the rush of adrenaline in my blood. I was a biker from that moment on.

The chilly Virginian mountain breeze quickly faded to a dry, hearty Nevada gust as I heard the moaning and groaning from the guys as they reached my position. I watched with a grin as they took turns pulling each other up and over the ledge where I was sitting. They were still huffing and puffing as they sat down beside me.

"Dammit, Turk!" yelled Stroker. "You and your fucking ideas. What are you trying to do, kill us?"

"Come on guys, we're not even to the top yet."

"Fuck that. This *is* the top as far as I'm concerned. We're waiting here for you," Hiney choked out.

"That's for damn sure," said Pegleg, wiping his brow.

"Hey, all right!" I said, throwing up my hands in defeat. "I'm fine right here."

Pegleg reached into his inner vest pocket and pulled out a hard pack of Marlboros. Flipping open the lid, he fingered through the cigs a moment before pulling out a joint. "Anyone care to partake?"

"Fire that fatty up," Stroker laughed.

Pegleg flipped open his Zippo and put the flame to the joint. He took a long drag and held it in as he passed it over to Stroker, who took a nice, long hit before handing it to Hiney. Pegleg coughed, spewing smoke from mouth and nose like a reefer dragon. I laughed watching Hiney inhale the fumes from the burning joint, trying his best to let it soak in his lungs before sputtering himself.

He also coughed his guts out as he exhaled. As he was choking on the smoke, he handed the blunt to me. I wasn't a smoker, but I took it from him anyway, just so he wouldn't drop it as he gagged. I usually didn't care to get high on grass, but in the moment, everything felt just right, and I wanted to join my bros on this "joint" adventure.

I inhaled, the smoke burning my throat and nose, and coughed it out almost immediately. The guys lost it in laughter. I tried handing it back, but they wouldn't have it.

"Keep it, Turk," Pegleg said. "You can do it! Give it another try."

He had to relight the joint for me, and I puffed, taking the fumes in for a second time. I didn't take as much this time, and it was easier to hold down. I slowly exhaled, relaxing into the wave of soft dizziness that enveloped me.

"Whoa!" I said, my breath a skunky puff. "Now that's some good shit."

I didn't actually know what good shit was, but it seemed like the right thing to say at the time. A single hit was enough for me, so I let the guys finish off the rest of the smoke.

We sat there on that fallen tree trunk laughing our asses off for the rest of the afternoon and almost killed ourselves trying to climb back down the mountain as the sun set behind the trees, throwing shadows on the loose rocks. It couldn't have been a better afternoon.

The sun had completely set by the time we made it back to the bottom of the mountain, dusty but alive. We were thirsty, and it was time to find a bar. We fired the bikes up and headed down the mountain, tearing through the quiet beauty of the scenic route with our stripped-down Harleys. We raced our way down the twisting roads and onto the highway, headed for Ernie's Bar.

Ernie's was located on the outskirts of Las Vegas and was one of our regular watering holes.

The four of us rolled up and immediately noticed two Harleys sitting in front of the saloon. Stroker took a long look at the bikes but didn't recognize them as anyone's we knew.

When we entered the pub, the bartender greeted us.

"What are you having today, boys?"

"Set us up with a pitcher of Bud and three glasses," said Hiney. "Hey Turk, you having a Jack and Coke as usual?"

I was too busy sizing up the two unknown bikers at the end of the bar to hear Hiney.

"Turk," Hiney said impatiently. "What are you drinking, man?"

Pulled out of my assessment by Hiney's grip on my shoulder, I irritably barked, "Jack and Coke, asshole!"

I probably didn't need to snap at him like that, but my high was wearing off, and I always prefer to know who's with me in a bar before I can relax.

As soon as we'd stepped through the door, I'd clocked them staring us down. They went back to their conversation when they noticed me eyeballing them.

The bartender set the drinks up on the bar, and I paid for the first round. I grabbed my Jack and headed for the back-corner table. My bros followed with their pitcher of beer, and we settled in where I could still keep an eye on the hunched figures of the unknown bikers.

When you wear a club patch, you're a different breed of biker. That patch tells everyone that your loyalty belongs to the club, and you trust no one outside your bros, not even other bikers. That's why I found it hard to meet new people.

Those patches are also why the cops think of us as outlaws. After the Hollister riot back in 1947, bikers were given a bad image by the media, despite the pervading theory that 99 percent of motorcyclists are law-abid-ing citizens. But it was that other 1 percent that were considered outlaws, which is why motorcycle gangs became known as One Percenters.

Even though most of us in the club didn't partake in illegal activities, we were all still guilty by association. So we kept the membership small, because it was safer and easier to keep track of everyone.

Hiney looked up from his glass, wiping the foam from his scruffy mus-tache, and saw me scrutinizing the bikers. Right away, he piped up with his nice guy bullshit.

"Huh — didn't notice those guys before. I haven't seen them around. Do you think they want to join us for a —"

"Hiney!" I yelled. "Have you lost your damn mind? You need to shut the hell up about them. I don't give a fuck about who they are! You got that?"

"Hey man!" Hiney said, throwing his hands up defensively. "It's cool! Calm down. With your attitude, it's a wonder we get any new prospects for the club."

"We don't *need* any new prospects," I said. "The club is already too big. If it were up to me, we'd get rid of a few of the idiots already in the club — and you'd be the first to go!" I slapped him jokingly upside the head.

I was only kidding, but Hiney didn't seem to get the joke.

"Fuck you, man!" Hiney grabbed his beer and walked away towards the bar.

"Damn, Turk," Stroker said turning to me. "You not just an asshole, you're a perfect asshole!"

I raised my glass and toasted Stroker and Pegleg. "He'll get over it."

I took a long swig, then looked over to see Hiney making conversation with the two saddle-bums at the end of the bar. Stroker saw my brow fur-row and quickly interjected.

"Cool it, Turk. It's no big deal," he said. "He won't do any harm. We both know he's just a lovable idiot. Let me get you another Jack. You want a double?"

I sat back in my chair and laughed, giving in to the obvious diversion. Stroker never bought drinks for anyone.

"Does this mean we're on a date?"

"Yeah, asshole," he said. "And if you buy dinner later, you might get lucky."

We all laughed, and my temper cooled.

"Pegleg, you better get the next round. I don't want Turk humping my leg," Stroker snorted.

"Sure, I'll just put it on Turk's tab."

I leaned back and took the last pull from the glass. "Go ahead. I love it when people owe me, because paybacks are a bitch."

I decided just to ignore Hiney. He knew how to piss me off, but he was one of my best friends. In fact, Hiney was the one responsible for introducing me to the club in the first place. I liked Hiney, and you always pick on the people closest to you.

The three of us sat back in our little corner shooting the bull. Our conversations usually revolved around tricks we've picked up on how to fix your Harley if it breaks down on the side of the road.

If you ride a Harley, you have to learn love working on it as much as you love riding it. When you build your bike from the ground up with parts you've made by hand in your garage, that Harley doesn't come with a warranty. Sure, those Japanese bikes might be more reliable, made and tested in a factory, but as the saying goes, I'd rather push my Harley than ride a Honda.

The regular bar customers filtered in and out throughout the evening, but we ignored them from our little spot of the world, which was just the way we liked it.

Eventually, Hiney made his way back to our table and sat down like nothing had happened. He didn't say anything to me, so I broke the ice.

"So Hiney, tell me something," I said. "On that recon mission of yours, did you find out who those guys were?"

"Yeah," he said, his voice betraying only a hint of defensiveness. "They're cool man. They just rode in from Reno for the weekend to check out Vegas. They're thinking about moving down here."

"What about that makes you think they're all right?"

"You gotta to decide that for yourself, Turk. I'm sure as hell not going to try and tell you what to think," Hiney took a long slug of his beer.

"Look man," I said. "You're one of my closest friends. I just think that sometimes you're a little too friendly for your own good. Know what I mean?"

"You're right. It's a shame we all can't be assholes like you, Turk."

I stood up and pulled Hiney into a friendly chokehold.

"Only my closest friends know what I'm really like, "I said, pretending to squint menacingly.

"Yeah, an asshole!" all three of my bros shouted at the same time.

"A toast to Hiney," I said, one arm still wrapped around Hiney's throat and the other raised in ceremony, "the nicest guy in the bar!"

We downed our drinks after I released Hiney so he could participate and slammed the empties on the tabletop. I had a great bunch of guys with me, and I felt honored to have them as friends.

The sun edged its way down into the horizon while we sat in a dingy little bar enjoying our dingy little lives far away from society's rules and judgment. We had just started to plan next weekend's ride when the bartender came over and planted four shots of Jack in front of us.

"From the two guys at the end of the bar," said the bartender, tossing his head in the general direction of the unfamiliar bikers. "I think they're getting ready to leave."

We held the shots in the air as a show of gratitude before slamming them down our throats.

"Thanks guys!" yelled Hiney.

They nodded back as they got their gear together and stood up. *What the hell,* I thought, and made my way over to thank them personally.

As I walked over, I noticed a grungy guy with fuzzy teeth staring me down.

I shot the stare back his way, thinking he'd look away, but his yellow eyes stayed steady on mine. I had almost made it to the visiting bikers when I stopped and turned, giving him a long, hard look.

"What," he barked, his lower lip bulging with tobacco.

I knew a challenge when I heard one.

"Keep looking at me and you're gonna find out *whut*." I stretched the last word with a dumb drawl, mocking his drooling tone.

The jackass didn't answer but turned and looked straight ahead at the mirror behind the bar. This guy really was stupid — he apparently didn't realize that I could see him still staring at me in the mirror. I guess the Jack got the better of me because I walked over and leaned in his face.

"My friends think I'm an asshole, and I'm trying my best not to be one right now, "I said. "How about helping me out by walking your ass out that door so I don't have to show you and everyone in this bar how big an asshole I really am."

The fucker just turned his head and snarled in my face, giving me an up-close look at the muck covering what teeth he had left. Before I could even wind up, Hiney had yanked him off the stool and into the air in a chokehold.

"You heard the man. You deaf or something?" Hiney growled into the mop of greasy hair.

Hiney dragged him over to the door, shoving it open with his captive's face before dumping the cretin unceremoniously in a puddle of garbage juice just outside. As the door slammed behind him, Hiney slapped his hands clean and said, "I've seen the asshole side of you enough today. It was my turn."

I laughed and threw my arm over his shoulder.

"Why don't you introduce me to your friends?"

When we turned to the guys at the end of the bar, they were wearing big grins of approval.

"I'm Smokey, and this is Motorman. Glad to meet you guys. I take it there's never a dull moment around here."

"You know, it's the damnedest thing — trouble just seems to find us," I said, shaking Smokey's callused hand. "Doesn't matter where we go."

"It couldn't just be your winning personality, now could it, Turk?" said Hiney, with a smile and a slap on my back.

"Anyway," I said, pointedly ignoring Hiney, "what brings you two to Vegas?"

"We've been here plenty of times to visit," Smokey said. "But we've been thinking we might just make Vegas home. I'm so fucking tired of Reno."

"Don't blame you," I replied. "Been to Reno a couple times myself. Don't much care for the cold. But Vegas is a good place for fellas like us."

With a friendly smile and a jovial smack on the arm, Motorman said, "Well, we better be getting on. We gotta check into our hotel. We have a room at that new hotel called the Landmark."

"All right guys," I said. "Ride safe."

No sooner had the door closed behind our new acquaintances did Smokey stick his head back in.

"Uh — you guys might want to get out here."

That tone said to move it. We rushed through the door and out into the parking lot. The sun had left behind a star-filled, amethyst twilight. In the fading light, I saw Motorman bent down beside my bike and I dashed over to him.

"This your bike, Turk?"

"Yeah, it's mine. Why? What's up?"

"Your spark plug wires are missing."

"What the fuck!" I felt the blood rush to my head and the heat rise in my throat. You don't fuck with a biker's ride — especially when that biker has a temper like mine. "Who the fuck fucked with my bike?!"

Smokey was standing with his arms crossed. He tossed his head in the direction of the trailer park across the street.

"When we came out, that dude your buddy threw out was leaning over your bike. When he saw us, he high-tailed it across the street," he said, his voice dripping with disdain for the vandal. He must have been real fucked up, because he fell on his face twice before he even made it down to that third trailer on the right."

Before he'd finished his sentence, I bolted across the street toward the dilapidated trailer. Through my haze of fury, I could hear Stroker and Hiney yelling for me to stop, but my blood was pounding in my ears and they were soon drowned out. I was too focused on my mission. All I wanted to do was get my plug wires back and then have a nice room arranged for that bastard at the hospital.

As I approached, I saw that the trailer was actually just a small pop-up camper hitched to the back of a pickup truck. I pounded on the door with everything I had, sure that my fist would go through the fiberglass with each thud. The curtains flickered open for a split second, then fluttered shut, but not before I caught a glimpse of the jaundiced eyes and greasy nose I was looking for.

I started kicking at the door, my steel-toed boots leaving scars and dents in the paneling. The rest of my bros ran up, the crunching of their boots on the gravel behind me alerting me to their presence. As they arrived, they too began pummeling the camper. We rocked the trailer back and forth until it threatened to tip over and screamed obscenities and threats loud enough for the entire trailer park to hear.

With a final grunt of empathetic anger, Hiney let loose his hold on the camper's frame. "Come on Turk," he said. "Let's get out of here before someone calls the cops."

"I'm not leaving till I choke the shit out of this asshole!"

"I know, bro . I want to choke him too," Pegleg said, crossing his arms. "But I don't want to go to jail over a set of sparkplug wires."

"Plug wires?" I yelled. "Screw that! That shithead fucked with my bike, and he's gonna fucking pay!"

"Hey, Turk!" Motorman shouted from the front of the beat-up pickup attached to the camper. "Check this out."

Motorman popped the hood the 1959 Dodge pickup and flicked out his Buck. He sliced through a couple of plug wires and held them up to me with a mischievous grin. "Here, these ought to get you home."

I took them from his outstretched palm and gave them a considering shake. I gnawed on my lip a moment before pulling my own knife out and slashing every visible wire under the truck's hood. Then, just for fun, I stabbed the upper radiator hose and watched it bleed green antifreeze all under the truck.

"Turk!" yelled Hiney. "That's enough! Let's go man!"

I walked over and smashed my fist against the camper door one final time.

"I'll be back, you motherfucker! I'll be back!" I roared before swiftly stabbing my knife through the mangled door. I strode away, leaving the hilt of my blade buried in the guy's camper as a reminder of what happens when you screw with a biker's Harley.

I crossed the highway at a fast trot. I knew we didn't have much time before the cops pulled up. As I replaced my stolen wires, I felt a tiny flicker of satisfaction. Two kicks later, my Harley was running. As she growled happily beneath me, my blood cooled and the ringing in my ears faded. I looked at Smokey and Motorman and smiled.

"Come on," I said. "We'll give you an escort to your hotel."

"Right on!" yelled Smokey.

"Bike sounds good," said Motorman, pulling alongside me. "Maybe I should get a set of truck wires for my bike."

With our Harleys roaring loudly, we threw loose gravel into the air and fish-tailed our bikes out of the parking lot before regaining traction on the asphalt. Four gears later, we were on our way to the strip.

As we rode through the neon-lit streets of Vegas, I looked in my mirror back at Motorman and Smokey. *Maybe I could stand to be a bit friendlier,* I laughed to myself. Tonight, our new pals were drinking on us.

CHAPTER 8

A LONG NIGHT

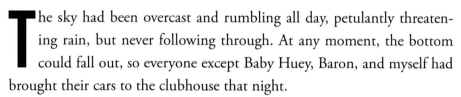

The sky had been overcast and rumbling all day, petulantly threatening rain, but never following through. At any moment, the bottom could fall out, so everyone except Baby Huey, Baron, and myself had brought their cars to the clubhouse that night.

The club meeting was short and to the point — business as usual. After the meeting was finished, the three of us sat on our bikes and watched the vehicles leave one by one until we were finally alone in the quiet front yard.

"Ya know," I said. "It's still early. Why don't we take a putt down to the Red Rock Saloon?"

The Red Rock Saloon was in Sloan, Nevada about 12 miles south on Las Vegas Boulevard, so it was a good spot to go to when we wanted to distance ourselves a bit, but not make a full run out of town.

"Yeah," Baron said, standing up in agreement. "That sounds good. I'm in! How about you, Huey?"

"Yeah, why not?" Huey answered with a shrug. "As long as Turk's buying."

"You're too easy, Huey," I said. "Let's get this show on the road."

"I'm ready! Just one for the road," Baron said, swigging from his vest pocket vodka.

With a swift kick, my Harley came alive. It was like a shot of adrenaline to my heart.

The clubhouse was off Nellis Boulevard by Sunrise Mountain. There was nothing out there but Nellis Air Force Base and a lot of empty desert to ride through — the perfect spot for a biker clubhouse.

We could just barely make out the faintest rays of desert sunset struggling to break through the heavy clouds as we flew through the city. Heading south down the Strip, we made our way past the Thunderbird Hotel, which was owned by the same people who owned the hotel I worked at.

Everyone knew Vegas was run by the Mob, and I liked the idea of working with them. I was the Valet manager at the Mint Hotel Downtown, and I took special care of the bosses' cars.

After the big bosses arrived each morning, I'd take their cars down the street and get them washed, gassed up, and serviced, as needed. When they came out at the end of the day, I'd run over, start the vehicles and drive them under the canopy. Starting a boss's car could be risky business back then, but it was all part of the job. They appreciated the dangerous favor and always took good care of me.

Working 9 to 5 Monday through Friday gave me plenty of freedom to be with the club. Plus, the Mint Hotel had no problem with my long hair and beard, and as the manager, I took as much time off from work as I needed and made great money.

One of the highlights of my job was the Mint 400 Race every year. The day before each race, the vehicles would parade down Fremont Street and go through the tech and safety inspection and be assigned a class. Once they passed the inspection, they were sent directly to the impound area.

I oversaw the impound-parking area, which gave me the opportunity to check out every truck and dune buggy in the race. I had the pleasure of meeting many great drivers like Mickey Thompson, Parnelli Jones, Rick Mears, and musician Ted Nugent. I would wait till no one was around and sit in their cars and imagine how it felt blasting through the desert in one of these hand-built monsters of the sand.

I often felt really lucky to have such a great job that offered me good benefits, awesome pay, and total freedom to run the show. Not to mention, it gave me plenty of time to ride with my bros on perfect nights like this.

It was late September, and the desert air was unusually humid, clinging to our skin as we pushed through the thick dampness. The valley was lit up as the neon lights of the Strip reflected off the low-lying clouds. We shot past the Thunderbird Casino, heading south, enjoying the smell of the cool damp air. Once we went past the bucking bronco sign of the Hacienda Hotel, we were officially out of town and the feeling of freedom we all felt was almost palpable.

Twenty minutes later, we pulled onto the crunching gravel of the Red Rock Saloon's parking area and shut our motors down. The night air was instantly filled with country music from the open bar door.

I stepped off my Harley, stretching my back and pulling in the scent of beer and late evening dew into my nose. I stepped up onto the wooden porch of the saloon and turned to see if my bros were behind me, but they were still standing at their scoots. Baron was taking a slow, gulping slug from his stash as Baby Huey looked on, shaking his head.

"You know Baron, they have plenty of that shit inside."

There was a beat of angry silence before Baron barked, "Mind your own fucking business, asshole! You want to be my mommy now?"

"Keep talking shit and I'll send you crying to your mommy."

"You stepping up? You want a piece of me?" Baron slurred, pushing into Huey's face. "Or you gonna hide behind that prez patch of yours like you always do?"

Like a shot, Baby Huey snatched Baron up by his throat with both hands, picking him off the ground by his neck.

"Which piece of you do you want me to start with first?" Huey growled.

Baron was trying hard to break Huey's hold on his neck, but it looked as if he was going to run out of air before that happened. I didn't want to deal with this bullshit and made my way back over to them.

"Hey, give me a fucking break!" I yelled. "Let him go, Huey!"

"Stay out of this, Turk," Huey spat over his shoulder at me. "This doesn't concern you."

"Everything that happens in this club is my business!" I grabbed Huey by the arm. "How many times do I have to tell you guys that? Now, are we going inside for a drink or did we come all the way out here just to fuck each other up?"

Narrowing his eyes, Baby Huey released Baron, dropping him to the ground in a heap. Baron looked up at Huey, rubbed his neck, and started scratchily laughing.

"That all you got, Huey?" He looked all right, but his voice was noticeably choked.

"I'm going inside for a drink before I do something I might regret later," Huey said, sounding tired. He pushed through the door, letting it swing shut swiftly behind him.

"Come on inside, Baron," I said, offering him a hand up from the dirt. "I'll buy you some vodka."

"Guess I showed him, huh?"

Baron and I walked into the red adobe bar and paused a moment at the door to check out the place. The wooden bar to the left along the wall was in dire need of a refinishing job, cracked and ringed from decades of wet glasses. To the right were four tables with a hodge-podge of chairs that all looked as old as Huey's '48 Panhead. The jukebox was sitting in the far back corner by the men's room and looked as if it was the newest addition to the bar. The walls looked like they probably had the original stucco on them from the early '50s, and some spots were cracked so bad you could almost see through to the outside.

I had been here on several occasions and this was my kind of place — the kind that said to each patron, 'you get what you get here'.

I looked back over to the bar at Baby Huey, who already had a frosty, full pilsner glass in front of him.

"You owe the bartender 50 cents for the beer," said Huey, taking a sip and walking past me with a grin.

The bartender looked at me like I was holding things up, even though we were the only ones in the bar. He had his head tilted, his arms heavily crossed, and an impatient expression on his mug. If I could have seen his feet behind the bar, I'd have been sure he was tapping one.

"There a problem?" I asked, walking up.

"No problem," he answered in a froggy voice, his expression unchanged. "I just need the money for that man's beer."

"Well, as soon as you set up a Jack and Coke for me and a double shot of vodka for my friend, I'll see what I can do," I said. "Where's Jake, the regular bartender? "

"He quit. Heard he got a job in town," said the bartender. "I just started this week."

I waited a moment to see if he'd start moving toward the bottles, but he stood unmoving. "Do you work for tips?" I asked, leaning against the bar.

"I sure do."

"Better start acting like it. In fact, let me give you a heads up. We'll be coming in here every so often, so if you take care of us, we'll take good care of you," I explained. "And if you don't take care of us, well, we'll take care of you. Catch my drift?" I raised my eyebrows emphatically.

"Yeah," said the barkeep, uncrossing his arms and jumping to grab a couple glasses. "It's cool, man."

"Yeah, I know it's cool," I said lightly. I wasn't about to start something over nothing. He caught me in a good mood.

He set my Jack and Coke down in front of me and slid a rock glass of vodka over to Baron as he walked up behind me.

"That'll be $4.25 total."

I put a $20 bill on the bar and slid it over towards him. "Let me know when that's gone."

I looked over at Baron to see him down the double shot of vodka and slammed the shot glass upside down on the bar top.

"You want a beer back with that shot, bro?"

"Nope, I'll be fine after a few more of these," he said, tapping the up-turned glass.

"Are you celebrating something or trying to get over something? "

"What do you fucking care, Turk? We all have our demons, right?"

"Yeah, but I deal with mine face-on. I don't hide inside a bottle of vodka because they'll just be waiting on me when I crawl back out."

"Well, whatever works for you," he said, pulling his bottle from his vest pocket and unscrewing the grin. "This works for me."

He downed another large swig of vodka and let out a loud gasp to clear his throat.

The barkeep saw him but wisely decided that it was in his best interest to just let it go.

"You know we're not that close to home," I said. "Slow it down a bit. And don't you dare call me your mommy. You know exactly what I mean."

Still, I signaled for the bartender to come back over.

"Set him up, again."

I didn't think Baron needed to be pounding them back like the world was ending, but I wasn't going to cut him off or anything. I knew the three of us could get one another home, no matter what kind of shape we were in.

"I'll have another," Huey called from a table, raising his empty glass.

"Lemme get you a fresh glass," the bartender said.

"Let's check out the box, Turk," Huey said, walking up and grabbing his beer.

With drinks in hand, we sauntered over to the jukebox.

"Pick a song, Turk."

I scanned the 45-rpm labels and figured the best I could do was "Crazy" by Patsy Cline. The sticker on the box said 3 plays for a quarter. I dug deep into my pocket and came up with 7 cents.

"You're going to have to do the honors, Huey," I said. "Do you have a quarter?"

Baby Huey came up with a couple pennies and a dime and smiled.

"Damn man, we don't even have a quarter between us. How sad is that?"

I laughed and shouted, "Baron, you have a quarter on you?"

Baron plunged his hands deep into his pockets and pulled out a fistful of coins, slamming them on the bar.

"Yeah, I got quarters. But not for no fucking country music, you got that?"

"Well, get your ass over here and pick out something you want to hear."

Baron picked out a couple of quarters from the bar top and made his way over to us. He threw his arms over both of our shoulders, and the three of us huddled over the box like we were planning a strategy. Only minutes ago, Huey's hands had been squeezing the air out of Baron's throat. But here we were, standing as brothers like always.

"You know, this is going to sound stupid," I confessed. "I hate country music, but I love Patsy Cline."

We all laughed in agreement and punched in her play numbers. The 45 was pulled from its slot and laid onto the turntable. The arm rotated over the record, and the lint-covered needle found its way into the first groove. After a few pops and cracks from the record dust, the song began to play. We all nodded in approval and headed back over to the bar.

"I saw Lance cruising down the road on his bike the other day," said Baron, pulling a stool under himself. "Have either of you heard from him since he left? It's been what, a couple months now?"

"Fuck no," I said, punctuating my sentiment with a sip of my Jack and Coke. "He doesn't give a rat's ass about us."

"That's where you're wrong, Turk," said Huey. "He's been calling me every week to see how we're doing."

"No shit! Really? What's he been doing?"

"He loves this chick, but he misses the club," said Huey. "He's confused right now."

"That's not good enough. If he's waiting to see what this chick will let him do, we don't need him around."

"Just because some broad's got him wrapped around her finger doesn't make him a bad guy," Baron replied. "You're taking this shit too personal, Turk."

"Well, you know what they say," I said. "Women are like hurricanes. They come into your life quickly, and when they leave, they take the house and everything else with them."

"I take it you're still pissed off about your divorce," laughed Baron.

"Don't push it, Baron," I snarled.

I didn't realize the Patsy Cline song had ended and silence had fallen. I was too absorbed thinking about how it ended with Melanie. I was 19 and in the military, and her parents had my 16-year-old wife convinced that I wouldn't be the same man when I came home. She filed for divorce a month before I was to leave for Vietnam.

Lance's problem with the club and my deal with my ex-wife were two completely different things. I didn't hang my dirty laundry out for the whole club to see.

As the night wore on and the conversations slowed, I was itching to hit the road and get to sleep.

"Hey, let's ride out to Jean and check out Bonnie and Clyde's car," Baron said, his eyes lighting up.

"Are you kidding me?" I asked incredulously. "You're too drunk to even keep your eyes open, let alone hold your bike up. The only place we're headed is home!"

"Fuck that! I'm gonna ride out to Jean and have a couple more out there."

"No, you're not. You've had four or five doubles here and half the pint in your vest. I think we should try and make it home, now."

"Man, I don't need your permission to do anything. I'm going to Jean whether you guys go or not."

I looked at Baby Huey for help, but all he did was shrug.

"You know, Baron. You're right," I said, turning back to him. "Do whatever the fuck you want to do, but I'm heading back to town. How about you, Huey? Where are you headed?"

"I'm going to finish this beer and head home," he said, staring at Baron.

Shaking his head, Baron grabbed his fingerless gloves off the bar and stormed out of the open bar door.

After he had dropped down on his pan's kick-starter lever six or seven times, we heard him yell, "Fuck!"

"He's too fucked up to even start his own scoot," I laughed to Huey.

The next kick brought his bike to life. With a quick twist of the throttle, the bike spun out of the driveway, throwing dirt and rocks at the front porch.

"He's a stubborn son-of-a-bitch, isn't he?" Huey sighed.

He picked up his beer and chugged the last half down. I was still staring out the front door, watching the cloud of dust slowly settle to the ground. I barely heard what Huey had said. My mind was miles away.

"Do you think we should go after him, or what?" I asked.

"Fuck no!" Huey shouted. "Not unless you want to spend the night in Jean. And if Baron has any sense, that's what he'll do."

"Yeah, but he doesn't have any sense. You're probably right, though," I said turning back to where Huey sat. "Let's have one more and call it a night. What d'ya say, Huey?"

"You trying to get me drunk and take advantage of me, aren't you, Turk?"

"You never complained before, bitch."

"Hey, set us up again," Huey yelled over his shoulder to the bartender.

Time slipped by, and we headed for the door a little later than planned. We had just walked through the door to our bikes when the ambulance went screaming past, heading south. My stomach dropped as I looked at Baby Huey.

"What do you think, Huey?"

"I don't know, man. I hope not," he said, reading my thoughts.

I threw my leg over my bike and stared south toward Jean.

"I don't know about you, man, but I'm not going to be able to sleep until I talk to Baron," I said.

"I know, I know," Huey sighed. "Let's get this over with."

About six minutes down the highway, we saw the flashing red lights in the distance. My mouth tasted sour and my stomach jerked.

Coming up on the scene, we slowed down and saw a Nevada Highway Patrol unit in the median as an officer directed traffic around the ambulance parked in the middle of the right lane. We pulled over behind the NHP vehicle and waited for the officer to approach us. I was hoping he would get pissed and flag us on past, but he didn't. As he approached, he gave us a long look, his eyes going to the club patches on our vests.

He stood silently for a moment before gently saying, "I'm sorry guys. He didn't make it."

I thought I'd imagined what he said, and shook my head numbly, trying to dislodge whatever waking dream the Jack and Cokes had created. I looked over at the ambulance in a daze. They were loading a body covered in a white sheet into the back. My blood roared in my ears as I stepped off my bike and ran over to the ambulance, Huey hot on my heels.

"Let us see him, man," Huey yelled, pushing past an EMT to look through the back window. "Let us see our bro!"

"Hey!" the ambulance driver shouted over Huey's clamor. "You guys need to step back."

"Fuck that!" I spat. "Show him to us!"

I was ready to climb in the back of the ambulance and punch the driver when the officer stepped up and put his hand on my shoulder. His grip was patient, but strong.

"Go ahead and let them identify him for me," he said. The paramedic looked at the cop and hesitantly nodded. He reached over and slowly pulled the sheet back.

"Damn it!" I screamed, feeling a vein in my forehead pulse. "No fucking way! He was just with us! Baron, you fucking asshole!"

Baby Huey grabbed me by the belt and gently pulled. I resisted, but Huey's soft voice brought me back.

"Turk, calm down," Huey said in a gentle, calming voice. "Come on, man."

I paced around to the front of the ambulance, punching into the air blindly, trying to release the electrifying aggression and guilt that was coursing through me. That's when I saw Baron's bike lying on its side by the edge of the road. I dropped to my knees beside it. The swirling red lights and rusty, metallic smell made me feel dizzy and sick, like I was stuck on a tilt-a-whirl. The chatter of emergency crews and gritty rumble of rubbernecking cars howled like a storm in my ears until I couldn't take anymore. I leaned over, retched, and my stomach emptied on the gravel in front of me.

Suddenly, there was a cold hand reaching under my arm and pulling me up. Baby Huey's eyes were as red as I had ever seen them.

"Come on, Turk. We need to get back to town. We have a lot of things to take care of." Huey's usually steady, soothing voice was ragged and hitching.

"I'm not leaving Baron until the ambulance takes him away."

"Okay, man. We'll stay here until they drive off."

We sat down a few feet from the bike and my puddle of vomit. After what felt like hours, the highway patrolman from earlier walked up and stared down at us. From my peripherals, I could tell he was holding something, but I stayed staring out into the dark desert, willing the nightmare to end.

"According to those two," he said, motioning to an older couple that was walking away from us toward their car, "your friend overshot the exit at a high speed and hit the gravel on the side of the highway. His bike fishtailed and slid down the road at about 80 mph with him pinned under it. I'm pretty sure I know what caused all this."

The officer held up a nearly empty bottle of vodka.

"This was found in his vest," he said. "Didn't even break after all that."

I took the bottle from the officer and stared at it. In the glint of the swirling lights reflecting on the neck, I saw Baron's glazed eyes as he twisted off the cap and took a long, gulping swig from the bottle.

"I believe that," the cop said, pointing judgmentally to the vodka, "was a major contributing factor in this accident."

"Is that a fact?" I murmured to the cop's reflection.

I stood up and cocked my arm back, then tossed the culprit as far out into the desert as I could. We all watched as the bottle faded into the thick black of the moonless night before a faint shatter sounded in the distance.

"Well, guess what? You've got nothing!"

Baby Huey and I pushed past the highway patrol officer, who made no move to stop us, and walked back across the highway to our bikes. I squatted down by my bike and looked up into the dark sky as fat droplets began to fall. The rain stung my cheeks as it fell harder and harder.

Huey and I leaned against our bikes in the rain as a tow truck pulled up and hauled Baron's mangled Harley from its desert grave. We stayed until the ambulance pulled away silently into the night without its emergency lights or siren blaring.

The highway patrol officer gave us one more glance before he drove away.

Then we were alone in the dark, standing noiseless and unmoving as the rain soaked through our clothes. We stood there, sodden and statue-like, holding silent vigil over this mortal spot in an immortal landscape. Our grief for our fallen brother could have held us there forever, but we had unpleasant business to take care of.

"It's time to go, Turk," Baby Huey said, the warmth of his hand on my shoulder unfreezing me from my requiem.

"Yeah, I know."

As I sat up from my bike, my legs buckled. Huey grabbed me, and I held onto him, taking several deep breaths before patting him on the back.

"Thanks, man," I said. "I'll be all right."

We ran hard through the storm, charging down the inky, glistening highway as the rain stung our bodies like thousands of needles. It was a constant reminder that this was real; it had happened. A few times I checked my mirrors, expecting to see Baron riding behind us, but there was only pitch darkness. But I could almost hear the thunder of his engine and see him in the corner of my eye, and it was comforting.

We were still a mile or two out of Vegas when the storm clouds parted. The rain let up and the air was thick with the smell of oil and asphalt. As we rounded the final bend, the neon lights of Vegas filled the skyline. It felt as though we carried our dark news like a cloud of black smoke to snuff out the incandescent glow. But when a bro dies, bleak sadness is felt deeply, but briefly. The grief would soon would come a party — a party to celebrate the life of Baron.

CHAPTER 9

HUEY'S ANNOUNCEMENT

There's got to be a better way to make a living, I thought to myself as I pulled my Harley into my garage. I unhooked my skidlid and tossed it over onto the workbench. It bounced across the wooden top, then dropped to the floor. I looked at it a moment, then decided that was a good place for it right now. I normally liked my gig as valet manager at the Mint Hotel Downtown, but this wasn't one of those days. Some days it could just really wear you out, physically and mentally, and my hangover from the party last night in celebration of Baron's life definitely didn't make it any easier.

The phone was already ringing when I walked into the house. I hesitated a moment and considered ignoring it, but the incessant mechanic shrieking grated on my frayed nerves and made my migraine pulse behind my eyes. I yanked the phone off its cradle on the kitchen wall.

"Yeah, what's up?" I barked.

"Hey, Turk," Cecil's voice cheerfully responded. "You busy? I wanna talk to you about something."

"No, I'm not busy," I said more calmly. Cecil's a good friend and hearing from him eased my irritation from work. "Always got time for you. What's up?"

"Well, I'll come right to the point," he said. "How would you like to be in a Clint Eastwood movie?"

"Wait, what? What's the deal?" I don't know what I'd been expecting him to say, but it hadn't been that.

"Well, I'm not sure," he said. "A detective from the gang unit came into my shop today asking about local clubs. He wanted to know if I could round up about 30 bikers for a shoot here in Vegas for an upcoming Clint Eastwood film."

"No, shit … What did you tell him?"

"I told him I couldn't, but I knew a guy who probably could. I told him about you and he asked me for your number, but I said no."

"Good," I said, relaxing a bit. "It was probably a scam to get information about our club."

"I don't think so, Turk. This seemed legit. I got his number and said I'd have you call him. That OK?"

"Sure," I said. "Give me the number, and I'll check it out."

"Make sure you call him, Turk!" Cecil said emphatically. "You wanna be in a Clint Eastwood movie, right?"

"Of course!" I said. "I can't let Dirty Harry down."

I wrote down the guys number and set it on the counter top as I hung up. I stood looking at the numbers on the slip of paper, just thinking. I wanted to give this some thought before jumping the gun. I walked to the fridge and popped open a bottle of Bud, taking a swig and staring across the kitchen where the slip of paper sat waiting. It only took a few minutes for my curiosity to get the best of me.

Screw it, I thought. I picked up the phone and dialed the number.

"Detective Ortoff speaking, how may I assist you?"

"I heard you're looking for some bikers to be in a movie with Clint Eastwood," I asked. "Is that true?"

"You must be Turk. Cecil said you'd be calling."

Dammit, Cecil, I thought. *You gave a gang cop my name?*

"So, what's the deal?" I asked gruffly.

"Mr. Eastwood is shooting some scenes for his new movie here in Vegas, and one of the scenes requires about 30 bikers."

"So, how do you fit in to all of this?"

"I'm with the gang unit here in Las Vegas. I guess they figured I'd know some up-and-up bikers suitable for the shoot," Detective Ortoff explained. "But in my line of work, I'm really more acquainted with more, shall we say, nefarious motorcyclists. Cecil said you'd be able to help me out. Do you think you can get that many bikers together with a few girls for the scene?"

"Sure! No problem. When do you need us?"

"Well, I'd like to take a look at you guys first to make sure you're what they're looking for. Do you have any pictures of your friends?"

"Yeah, I have tons of pictures."

"How about I stop by and check them out?"

"Sure. Come by after 5 tomorrow. I'll be waiting."

"Thanks, Turk. What's your address?"

"Come on, man. If you're with the gang unit, you're most likely looking at it right now."

He laughed. "Ok, Turk. See you tomorrow."

I didn't want to tell anyone that a member of the gang unit was coming to my house until I was sure the movie deal was solid.

The guys and I had a shot at becoming a part of the legacy of Clint Eastwood classics. I was thrilled at the thought of meeting Dirty Harry in the flesh, but I had to restrain myself until I was sure this was legit.

I had the album of the club pictures ready on the dining room table when Detective Ortoff appeared at my door the next afternoon.

After our short greetings, we pulled up a chair to the table and opened the album. With each page he flipped through, his smile widened.

"These guys are perfect!" he said excitedly.

"When and where do you want us and what does it pay?"

He pulled out some intimidating documents and read them for a moment before smiling and looking up at me.

"It pays $275 a day for each of the bikers and $150 a day for each of the girls. How's that sound?"

"Shit, that sounds great! I probably shouldn't tell you this, but I would have done it for free!"

I was blown away. My house payment was $262 a month, and I thought that was high.

"Detective Ortoff, you just bought yourself a bunch of bikers."

The detective wrote down the date and time we were to meet the crew and said he would touch base with me a couple times before the shoot to make sure we were still on the same page. I saw him to the door and watched as he climbed into his unmarked car. I couldn't figure out if I was helping the cops or if they were helping us. Either way, we were going to be in a Clint Eastwood movie.

A couple nights before that week's club meeting, I called Baby Huey and told him to make this week's gathering mandatory, because I had something important to discuss. I needed everyone to call their contacts to make sure that absolutely everyone was there.

A few years back, we set in motion a policy that enabled us to keep tabs on all our members. Each member had two other members' numbers to call every morning, just to touch base. That way, we all knew immediately if someone was missing, arrested or in the hospital. It was a good system, and it worked.

The night of the meeting finally arrived, and I told Baby Huey to take care of the normal club business first. I wanted to save what I had to say for last.

Maybe I was just excited, but Huey seemed a little long-winded that night and I was getting very impatient. I was feeling extra antsy and was about to tell him to hurry it up, when he dropped the bomb. He wanted to step down as club president and have the club vote on whether Doc, the vice president, should take his place.

I knew Baby Huey had been going through some surgery to help his old war wounds, but I never realized it would take such a toll that he'd want to step down. Back in Vietnam, he'd been so pumped full of lead that they didn't even bother checking to see if he was alive and just laid him in the row of dead bodies from the assault. He sure scared the shit out of them when he came to, screaming and gurgling from the pile of corpses! All those years in and out of the VA Hospital were finally taking their toll on the crazy bastard.

"I'm not leaving the club," Huey said over the clamor of dissent. "I'm still gonna be a member, so keep your shirts on. I love you guys, but it's just that I can't concentrate on anything right now but my health. I need you all to understand this."

I looked over to Doc who was sitting stone-faced on the couch. He seemed entirely unsurprised by Huey's announcement. I guess they'd been discussing this for some time. Baby Huey walked over and flopped down onto the couch.

"You know," Huey said, playfully nuzzling himself deeper into the stained cushions, "it feels good already just being one of the guys."

We all laughed, but a cloud of disappointment settled over the room.

The vote was unanimous. Doc walked over and sat in what had been Huey's chair.

"I know I've got some big shoes to fill," he said. "But you guys know me. I'll do my best for the good of the club. I think my first order of business is to elect a new Vice President."

I put my hand up and looked at Baby Huey.

"No, Turk. I don't want the honor, please. In fact, I'd like to nominate Big Dave. Are there any objections?"

No one could argue with that. Big Dave was a dedicated club member. He was an iron-worker and a big man to reckon with. Big Dave was voted in unanimously, and Doc continued with the business at hand.

"Turk," Doc said. "I understand that you have something to bring to the table."

I stood up and clapped my hands together. "Well guys, it looks like we have hit the big time! Clint Eastwood is filming a movie in Las Vegas, and he wants us to do a scene with him. Any takers?"

The room erupted with a bunch of maniacs yelling and hollering. Some were in disbelief and others screaming about being movie stars. Once I convinced everyone it wasn't a joke, the questions started flying.

"Do we get to kick Dirty Harry's ass?" Pegleg yelled.

"He's not Dirty Harry in this movie," I explained. "He plays an expendable cop from Phoenix who needs to pick up a witness in Vegas, someone both the mob and the cops want to kill."

Needless to say, it didn't take too much convincing. I gave the dates and time to Doc, so he could plan our calendar for this event. After the meeting, I walked up to Baby Huey and stood looking at him.

Without saying a word, we embraced with a large pat on the back in friendship and brotherhood.

"You know, Huey, I'm gonna miss you being the boss."

"Bullshit!" he said. "You hate anyone telling you what to do."

"Yeah, but I hated you the best."

We laughed and walked out to our scoots. I sat on my bike and looked over at Huey.

"It was an honor riding next to you on our rides."

"Knock it off, Turk. I always had to make you ride up front with me."

"I know, I know," I said. "It just feels weird that you're not in charge anymore. I'm going to miss arguing with you."

"That's it, Turk!" Huey said, pumping up the starter pedal. "Now you're buying the first round."

As we rode through the streets of Las Vegas to our favorite watering hole, I couldn't help but stay slightly to the right of Huey's rear tire. I had to wonder what direction the club would take with Doc as president. I watched Baby Huey maneuver his rigid Panhead in front of me and realized it was the end of an era for this club, and I wasn't happy about it.

When we arrived at the Backstreet Tavern everyone was gathered outside, waiting for Baby Huey and me to arrive. They wanted to escort us in and buy us shots to celebrate.

I was high on adrenaline and excitement over the movie deal and told Hiney to hold the door open for me. I was still on my scoot, and he gave me a puzzled look. I gunned my motor and shot forward though the open door into the bar. Some guys cheered while others were shouting in confusion and disbelief.

I didn't give a shit. With my engine burning everyone's eardrums, I drove over to the waitress' station where I slid to a stop and revved my motor a few times. I shut down my engine and stared at the barkeep.

"I'll take a Jack and Coke."

"Get that thing out of here!" the bartender screamed maniacally. "The fire marshal will shut me down!"

"Not until I get my Jack and Coke."

"I'm not going to tell you again to get that fucking bike out of here."

"You better get me a Jack and Coke, or I'm going to kick your ass. And then I'm going to call the fire marshal myself and have him shut this fire trap down."

"You had best get him a Jack and Coke," Huey said to the bartender, giving me a slap on the back. "I promise that's the only way he's gonna move that bike."

With a pissed off look, he made a Jack and Coke and slid it down the bar to me. I grabbed the glass and took a drink before slamming it back on the bar and looking him straight in the eyes.

"I wanted a double."

I could almost see the veins in his neck popping out from under his collar. The bartender reached over and grabbed a bottle of Jack Daniels, setting it beside my drink.

"Keep the bottle," the barkeep yelled. "Now get that fucking bike out of my bar!"

I took the bottle and raised it over my head like a trophy as everyone cheered. I handed it to Baby Huey, who just smiled and shook his head. He reached down and grabbed the back of my hair, pulling his face down into mine.

"I don't care what you do anymore, Turk," Huey laughed. "Your Doc's problem now."

He let go of my hair and slapped me on the back of the head.

"Now get that bike out of here," Huey yelled.

"Come on guys, help me get this thing out of here."

As the guys pulled from the rear, we managed to get the bike back out into the parking lot. I walked back into the bar and took the bottle of Jack from Baby Huey. I raised the bottle over my head again, and once I got everyone's attention, I placed it back on the bar.

"Hey man," I said to the bartender. "I don't want your bottle. I was just having some fun. You know how fun can get very dangerous. Catch my drift."

"Yes, I do, very well. We're cool, man," he said rolling his eyes. This guy was used to our bullshit.

"Then how about making me that double so we can get this party started?"

I turned with my drink in hand and looked at everyone.

"We're going to be movie stars!" I yelled.

We raised our drinks and toasted to Clint Eastwood and his new movie, "The Gauntlet."

CHAPTER 10

THE GAUNTLET

I t was a chilly morning when I arrived at the meeting place the day of the shoot. I wanted to stand out in the crowd a little, so I wore my brown leather jacket with arm fringe under my vest. Everyone arrived around 8 a.m. at the parking lot of the Hush Puppy Restaurant on West Charleston, near Rainbow.

Rainbow Boulevard was a beat-up, two-line asphalt stretch that ran south across the desert from Fremont Street to Blue Diamond Road. It was as far west as any road in Vegas went. It was full of dips and washout areas caused by flooding from the mountains.

We stood around shooting the shit until one of Mr. Eastwood's assistants pulled up, and we followed him south on Rainbow to our destination. About a mile before Blue Diamond Road, we turned right on this pot-hole riddled, make-shift road. We bounced along down the mangled path a ways until I spotted some caves in the side of a mountain ahead.

Jeez, I thought, *how the hell did they stumble on a place like this in the middle of nowhere?*

It seemed like we rode for hours on that beat-up piece of shit road, barely able to do 15 miles an hour, while we dodged large rocks and small craters. I couldn't help thinking that it might've just been smoother to ride through the desert and avoid the road entirely.

When we finally pulled up to the site, I stood up and rubbed my numb ass. All those bumps and holes had vibrated my ass until it fell asleep. While I was still stretching and trying to wake my rear up, Mr. Eastwood walked around a large boulder, appearing like his cue had been called. Seeing the man himself walk up felt like I'd fallen into the movie screen; it was surreal and indescribable.

After greeting us and asking us to call him Clint, he walked over to talk with the cameraman. I didn't realize it at the time, but Clint Eastwood was the director as well as the lead. Since we were in the middle of nowhere, he had decided to only use one Panavision Camera and shoot each scene several times at different angles.

There were four other actors on the set with Clint. Sondra Locke played a prisoner that needed to be transported back to Phoenix, and there were two guys and a girl dressed as bikers to blend in with us. They did all the dialogue since no one in our group had Screen Actors Guild Cards. They also had two Knucklehead Harleys of their own to use for the scene.

Clint started by positioning all our Harleys in a circle around the scene area, then focused the camera at the cave from the center of the bikes. Then he joined Sondra Locke in the cave to begin the scene. It was like watching him flip a switch when he started to act. He wasn't Clint Eastwood anymore — he was Ben Shockley.

"All right you mother jumpers, this is a bust!" he shouted, descending from the cave with his gun aimed at our ranks.

Our scene was maybe 10 minutes long, but it took almost 10 hours to shoot. Between all the times the actors had to be fed their lines and the camera being moved to different positions for the same scene to be shot at a different angle, it took a damn long time. When we were about halfway through shooting the scene, we broke for lunch.

I had brought my girl Gloria with me to join in the crowd of extras, and as everyone else rushed to the lunch trailer, we stayed back. Gloria had to take her shoes off for a moment to rub her feet.

"I know how you feel," Clint said as he approached us. "My feet are killing me too."

"Standing on these rocks will take their toll on your feet," Gloria said, rubbing gingerly.

"They sure will," Clint said with an apologetic smile. "Hey, that's a mighty fine-looking bike you have there. Mind if I sit on her?"

"Go ahead," I said eagerly. "You'll be doing me an honor."

He straddled my bike, and I looked around to see if anyone else was watching this life-changing event, but we were alone. Everyone was already down at the roach coach.

"This is nice, real nice," Clint said, holding the handles. "How are you all holding up? I know it's been a long day already."

"We'll be fine," I smiled. Gloria nodded in agreement.

He smiled, knowing we were lying. "I guess I need to thank you guys for helping out."

"It's more like we need to thank you for letting us help out."

He grinned and stepped off my bike. "Let's get something to eat."

"Sounds like a good plan," I said.

Once Gloria had pulled her boots back on, we walked down the hill to the lunch wagon where everyone had gathered. The food was unbelievable — and from a food truck, no less! These people knew how to eat. Clint sat with Gloria and I, and it will be a lunch I will always remember. I mean, how many times do you get to have lunch with Clint Eastwood?

"So, why aren't you Dirty Harry in this film?" I asked after swallowing a big bite from a glistening, succulent fried chicken leg.

He chuckled. "No Dirty Harry this time. I play a worthless cop that is going to be sacrificed with a hooker."

"Any good love scenes in it for you, Clint?" I asked, waggling my eyebrows suggestively.

"Nah, we're too busy dodging bullets and beating up bikers."

"Tsk, too bad," I shook my head. "Someone needs to talk to the writer."

"Is that so?" he said, wiping his mouth. "You don't look like the romantic type to me, Turk."

The actors and my bros all shared a good laugh, and we finished our meal and conversations.

It was past 2 p.m. by the time we'd finished lunch and headed back up to the caves. We were all riding high from our once-in-a-lifetime lunch with Clint Eastwood and were rearing to go for the next part of the scene.

The next shot was of an argument between Clint's character and one of the biker actors. He threw the guy on the ground where the supposed-biker whimpered for mercy. With a bang, he shot a hole in the Harley's oil tank instead of the biker's head. The gunshot, of course, was all staged. The .44 Magnum shot blanks, so a small charge was put inside the tank, so it would explode as if it were really hit with a bullet. It was a cool scene, but I still hated seeing a Harley get shot, even if it was fake!

The last take was of us riding our bikes into and out of the scene area to be edited into the proper spots later on. Again they had to move the camera to different positions each time we came up the dirt road and down the dirt road, so it took quite a bit of time.

It was a pain in the ass navigating our machines around the rocks and potholes each time, but it was also a blast seeing Clint directing the cameramen on each of the shots, so I'd have done it another thousand times if he wanted me to.

The day was very long, but still ended way too quickly as we wrapped up the last shot. We headed back down to the trailer area and filled out the paperwork to get paid.

"You really made my day," I said, shaking Clint's hand.

"That's not one of my lines, is it?" he teased "But really, the pleasure has been all mine. I think what we did here today was just what we wanted. I want to thank all of you for your patience and stamina."

Clint's face filled with a grin, the one I have seen so many times on the big screen. He turned from me and shook everyone else's hand as the guys all lined up for their chance to be one-on-one with "the man." This was as much payment as the check!

Most of the guys wanted to party and celebrate our day with Clint Eastwood, but Gloria and I declined. The 12-hour day in the sun and dust was enough for me to call it quits and head home. The ride home was a natural high. It felt good just to relax on my bike as it rode down some smooth highway asphalt; I appreciated it all the more after the last couple hours of riding on potholes and rubble.

All I did after getting home was slip off my boots and throw my head on the pillow. But even as dead tired as I was, I still couldn't sleep. The excitement of the day was still coursing through me. I couldn't wait for the movie to come out. I fell asleep dreaming of my face on the silver screen.

The next morning, I was out taking care of some personal business and cruising up West Charleston when I saw a crowd of people standing on the side of the street. I pulled over to investigate and saw a film crew, including the cameraman from yesterday, setting up for another shot.

I pulled alongside some barricades to get a better look. The film crew was standing around taking a break, and Clint was nowhere in sight. I saw his small white trailer shimmy as someone inside moved around and figured he was inside.

I heard someone approaching and looked to my left to see a Clark County cop staring me down. I was illegally parked in front of the barricades, but, shit, I've definitely done worse.

"Hey, you can't park here!" the cop barked. "Move it!"

"I thought this was motorcycle parking!" I tossed him a shit-eating grin.

He stared back stone-faced. "It's not. Now, move that motorcycle out of here."

"How about you just write me a parking citation, and I stay."

The shocked look on his face was priceless. He had turned beet-red and was leaning into my face when the crowd started cheering.

We both looked over to the trailer where Clint Eastwood had appeared on the step.

"Hey Clint!" I shouted with a hand raised in easy acknowledgement.

It was a miracle that he heard me, but he did.

"Hey man!" he said with a smile of recognition. "How are you?"

Clint raised his hand in a friendly wave. That's all I needed to see. I nodded and kicked my bike off the kickstand. The crowd had turned to see who the lucky bastard was that was on speaking terms with Dirty Harry.

"Later dude!" I said with another smirk.

I dropped the transmission into first and roared off as the crowd looked on. I had to really play it cool. After all, I was a movie star now.

As I drove home with the V-twin vibrating though my bones, I couldn't help but think how different my life would be if I had never become a biker.

I had built my first motorcycle from farm scraps, but a man's first Harley is something else entirely. It changes you. From the very moment I kicked that bike into gear, Harleys filled my blood and soul. That bike changed me and became a part of who I was.

So when it was taken from me, I threw myself down a path I knew I might not come back from. Nothing and no one was going to hold me back from my mission.

1971

CHAPTER II

JACKIE'S RIDE

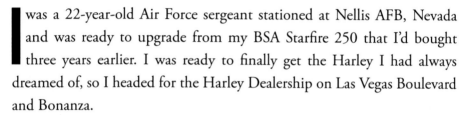

I was a 22-year-old Air Force sergeant stationed at Nellis AFB, Nevada and was ready to upgrade from my BSA Starfire 250 that I'd bought three years earlier. I was ready to finally get the Harley I had always dreamed of, so I headed for the Harley Dealership on Las Vegas Boulevard and Bonanza.

I walked in the front door and glanced around at the new 1971 Harleys on the showroom floor. The first one I saw was a stripped-down dresser with a Sportster front end. It was white with red and blue pinstripes around the Harley logo on the tank. The rear fender was shortened and squared off at the end, with a small round taillight. I didn't give it a second look.

The salesman came up with a smile and shook my hand.

"Anything I can help you with?" he asked.

I pointed to the bike by the front door.

"What kind of Harley is that?"

"That's a '71 Super Glide FX, customized straight from the factory. What do you think?"

"The front end is way too skinny for that bike," I answered. "It looks awkward."

"Yeah, I hear that a lot."

"What I really want to look at are your Sportsters," I said.

"Those are the only two I have left, "he said, pointing to a couple in the corner. "I won't be getting anymore till the '72 models come out in about 6 months."

The blue one caught my eye, and I walked over to get a better look.

"What do these run?" I asked, gliding my hand down the smooth, glinting paint job.

"They're $1,995 and worth every penny of it," he said. "Sit down and get a feel for her."

My heart thrummed excitedly as I threw my leg over her. I pulled her off the kickstand and held her upright. She was much larger and heavier than my BSA, and I could feel her power under me, even before her engine was roused.

"Well, how does she feel?" the salesman asked with a knowing smile. My thoughts must have been written on my face.

"She feels really good," I admitted. "Mind if I sit here a few minutes to think about it?"

"Take your time. Let me know when you're ready."

I sat alone in the showroom on that brand new 1971 XLCH Harley Sportster for over an hour. The bike had no chrome except what was on the air cleaner and gauges; the heads and casing were just polished, and the oil tank was black. I had seen a Triumph that was completely chromed out and cost $300 less just a few days back, but this one just felt right. I was still going back and forth between the two when the salesman returned.

"Well, what do you think?" he asked.

I smiled, leaned the bike back onto its kickstand and stepped back to give her another good hard look. There was no doubt about it.

"I'll take her!" I said emphatically. "Can you have her ready for me today?"

"No problem!" the salesman said. "Let me roll her back to the garage, and I'll be right back."

The Triumph was completely out of my mind. All I could think about was my new Harley. She felt like destiny.

As I waited for the salesman to return, my mind drifted back to the motorbike I had built on the farm with an old two-stroke motor and bicycle frame. I crashed it after one ride, but I was hooked. Here I was planning on buying a $2,000 Harley.

The salesman came back out and walked behind the wooden display case that separated the showroom from the service area. He pulled out some paperwork and laid it on the glass top.

"My name is RR, and I own this place," he said, shaking my hand. "And you are?"

"I'm Rick Hart."

"Well, if you'll just start filling out these forms for credit, we'll get things rolling here."

I stared at the form for a moment. I had no credit to speak of. My heart dropped into my stomach with an almost audible splash of anxiety.

"Look, RR," I said tentatively, "I just got stationed at Nellis Air Force Base. I have no credit references to list on the application, but I do have $1,000 to put down on it. If you finance the $995 balance, then we have a deal."

"So, you say you're in the military?" RR asked. "Do you have military ID?"

"I sure do."

I pulled the ID out of my wallet and handed it to him. He took a minute to look at it and then picked up my paperwork of the counter and tore it in half. "We won't be needing this."

My heart plummeted. My dreams of owning a Harley were shattered at that moment.

But then he said, "Your signature is good enough for me. Just fill out these papers, Mr. Hart," he said pulling out a new set of forms. "My shop will be glad to finance you."

"Thanks so much, RR!"

"I was also in the service. I'm glad to help out a fellow veteran."

By the time I had the papers filled out for RR, the mechanic had the bike serviced and ready to go for her maiden voyage. She was my first major purchase on my own, and I felt like I had passed the rites to manhood.

We walked out back and there she sat, my brand new '71 Sportster XLCH. She was the most impressive thing this Virginia mountain boy had ever seen. I looked down at the controls and hesitated, realizing I didn't actually have a clue how to start her. RR laughed and ran through the functions of each of the switches on the handlebars.

"I'd tell you how to start her," he said, putting the key in the ignition, "but each Harley has its own personality. Over time, you'll find the exact throttle and choke to use to get her going. For now, I'll show you the basics."

I was excited, and even though I had very limited experience on motorcycles, I felt like I'd owned her all my life. I couldn't wait to hear her start up.

I pulled the choke out halfway, turned on the gas, and pumped the pedal three times.

I turned the ignition on and primed the pedal for full compression, then down I kicked. Without hesitation, the motor roared to life. Damn, she felt good between my legs.

"Be very easy the first 500 miles to break everything in, " RR said, putting his hand on my shoulder. "After that, bring her in so I can check everything out."

"Thanks, RR," I said as I popped her into first gear. "I'll see you soon."

I pulled out of the parking lot and drove off into the next chapter of my life.

Cruising Fremont Street was a nightly ritual for me during the summer of '71. The bright lights of the downtown casinos like the Golden Nugget, The Horseshoe, The Fremont, the Four Queens, and The Mint attracted young people like fireflies.

Fremont Street was cruised from Las Vegas Boulevard to Main Street where they ended in a small park where you could circle back down. There was a continuous flow of vehicles traveling up and down the strip each night.

A lot of bikes also made their way through the traffic of Fremont Street, and I was one of them. My best friend, Bill, had bought the other Sportster that was left at RR's shop the minute he saw mine. We always rode together, so we got the nickname, "The Sportster Brothers."

One summer night, Bill and I were cruising Fremont Street when we decided to park in front of McDonalds. It was a great spot to just sit and watch the parade of cars and crowds go by. Among the crowds there were always plenty of girls, too.

I had installed a three-pronged sissy bar on the rear fender of my Harley and had wrapped it with my military blanket. I liked to lean back on my sissy-bar, prop my legs up on my passenger pegs and watch the show on the strip.

Fremont was packed tonight, and the cars were barely moving. That's when I saw her. She was alone in the backseat of an old Rambler with two other girls up front.

I jumped off my bike and walked through traffic to get a better look. As I made my way through the slow-moving cars to her, our eyes met, and I fell instantly in love.

I walked alongside their car as it moved inch-by-inch through downtown Las Vegas and tried to start a conversation with her.

"Hey, why don't you hop out of the backseat and come cruise the strip with me on the back of my Harley?" I asked in my smoothest voice. I flashed her a smile and heard her friends giggle.

"No thanks," she answered politely, but slightly taken aback. "I'm just fine back here."

I dodged oncoming traffic and gave it another shot.

"Come on," I pleaded. "We'll just go for a short ride, and I'll bring you right back. I promise."

My elbow was struck then by a passing vehicle's side mirror, sending my funny bone ringing numbly. The driver blasted his horn and shouted obscenities at me from his open window. I jogged to catch up to her car to find the girls hysterical with laughter.

"You better be careful," she said through her giggles. "You're going to get run over out there."

"Well, if you'll go for a ride with me, it might just save my life."

She bit her lip and smiled. Just when I was sure she was going to give in, the shriek of a police siren filled the air. I turned to see a brown and white cruiser pulling up along side of me in the oncoming lane.

Over the speaker, an irritated voice droned, "Get out of the middle of the street before I write you up for jay-walking."

"Sorry, officer. It won't happen again." I threw up my hands in apology and turned back to the Rambler.

The traffic had begun to move, but as the Rambler pulled away, she leaned out the window, waved, and smiled sweetly. My heart jumped into my throat. I stood in the middle of the street as horns blared and pedestrians pointed, but I could see only her as she disappeared into the maze of the traffic.

I made my way back to where my bike was parked and saw that a few more bikes had arrived. One of them was owned by a good friend of mine, Spider, a three-cylinder, two stroke Suzuki 500cc motorcycle. Spider and Bill were talking when I walked up.

"Any luck with that girl?" Bill asked with a grin.

"No, but I was almost run over for trying."

"A chick to die for, right Rick?"

I just nodded dazedly.

I settled down on my scoot again and tried to get back into my groove of watching the people on Fremont Street. But I found myself looking for that old Rambler. I couldn't get that smile of hers out of my head.

My heart had just started to slow when Bill's voice snapped me back to reality.

"Hey Rick, your girlfriend's here."

I whirled around. I couldn't believe my eyes. There she stood with that cute smile of hers.

"I'll take that ride now," she said, brushing her hair behind her ear.

I was entirely dumbstruck.

"Wow," I managed. "I didn't think you'd come back."

"I didn't think you'd make it out alive," she laughed.

I just stood there, caught up in her eyes. I was in shock that she was even standing there. After a moment, she broke the silence.

"You … wanted to take me for a ride?" she hinted. I must have looked as flabbergasted as I felt.

"I sure do!" I answered eagerly. "We can do that!"

I gently took her hand and walked her over to my bike.

"Give me a second to start her," I said.

I stepped over and gave my Harley two primer kicks. On the third stroke, I came down hard on the pedal. The bike just sputtered feebly. I glanced over my shoulder at her, smiled and kicked again. My Harley still didn't start, and I was getting embarrassed. The kicking continued for some time to no avail. I was getting tired, and the guys were of no use as they teased me with less and less regard for my swagger. I sat on my bike side-saddle to catch my breath. I took both her hands and pulled her towards me.

"I need to rest a minute. She might be flooded," I explained. "Now might be a good time to tell me your name."

"I'm Jackie, and I take it you're Rick?"

It hadn't been a hard mystery for her after the guys began chanting it repeatedly with each of my kicks.

"Yes," I breathed a laugh. "It's a pleasure meeting you, Jackie."

"What's wrong with your Harley, Rick?" Spider called. "Won't she start?"

They all laughed as I stood up to kick her again, filled with renewed drive.

"Let me try," Jackie said, laying a hand on my shoulder. "My dad rides Harleys, and he used to let me start them."

I could feel the guys' eyes on me and couldn't give up like that.

"No thanks, I can do this."

"Aw, come on, man!" Bill said. "Let her try."

Everyone started chanting, "Jackie, Jackie, Jackie …"

"OK, OK," I said, trying to keep from rolling my eyes. "Don't lock your knee out in case she kicks back. I don't want you to get hurt." I tweaked her chin and gave her a wink.

I stepped back as Jackie moved to the right side of the bike. With her left leg high on the pedal, she pushed her body up and came down hard. The engine roared to life and the crowd went crazy.

"One kick, man!" Spider shouted ecstatically. "She did it on one kick!"

"Way to go, Jackie!" Bill grinned. "Way to go!"

She walked up with a huge smile and wrapped her arms around my neck.

"I'm really sorry," she said, sounding not the least bit apologetic.

The tiny spark of annoyance I felt at the situation disappeared instantly as she leaned forward and lightly bit my ear, whispering, "Let's get the hell out of here."

I climbed on the rumbling Sportster and held my hand out for her to grab. She took it and swung her spectacular leg over the seat. Once she'd settled in, she wrapped both her arms tightly around my waist.

"Let's see what this thing can do," she said.

I smiled and nodded at my buddies. "I'll catch you guys later. Don't wait up for me."

I twisted the throttle, released the clutch and the Harley lunged out onto Fremont Street. We sped east down Fremont Street to Las Vegas Boulevard and turned right for the Strip.

After cruising a couple of blocks she said, "I thought you were going to show me what this thing could do?"

Well, that's a first, I thought. Girls usually are skittish going even slower than we'd been going. I grinned and shook my head. "OK, hold on!"

She was the first person to ride on the back of my Sportster, and she wanted me to punch it. I was pleasantly surprised by her request and certainly eager to please. I down shifted from 4th to 2nd and popped the clutch.

I was still new to the performance of its 900-cc engine so what happened next was a total surprise to me. The engine revved to red line, and the front wheel came off the ground as we lunged forward. I quickly shifted to 3rd gear, and the speed was pulling me back into Jackie. I had to dodge a few cars, but the road ahead was ours. At the red line, I found 4th gear and slowed the bike back down to 60 mph.

Jackie let out gleeful shout of exhilaration as we made our way down the strip with the wind ripping through our hair. When red lights appeared ahead, I backed off the throttle, settling into traffic.

"Now *that* was fun!" she laughed.

"I take it this wasn't your first ride on a Harley?" I asked.

"I told you that my dad rides Harleys. I used to ride with him a lot."

I nodded and slid down in the seat against her warm body. I was enjoying her arms wrapped tightly around my waist as we swerved in and out of traffic on the Las Vegas Strip. I pulled into Caesars Palace and putted slowly through the valet area just to piss the valet guys off after pealing back out onto the strip.

Heading north on the strip in the direction of downtown, I saw the Peppermill on the right and decided to stop.

"What are we doing here?" she asked.

"What kind of date would this be if I didn't even buy you a drink?" I said, shutting off the engine.

"I don't drink, Rick, but I'll have a soda."

"Wow," I said. "You just keep getting better every minute. Do you smoke?"

"No, do you?"

"No, but I have been known to have a cocktail or two. What about kids? You want to go halves on a kid?"

"Shut up," she laughed, slapping me on the chest.

We entered the restaurant and were seated in a booth. I slid in close to her and she took my hand under the table. Her warm thigh pressed against mine, and I let myself fall into her eyes. We sat there silently for a few minutes, just snuggling in the booth. She had me hook, line, and sinker, and I didn't care.

I told her about my time in the service and how I wanted to make Las Vegas my home after I was discharged. We talked and talked about anything and everything.

"So, you say your dad rides a Harley. You still ride with him?"

"No, not since my mom divorced him. I actually live with my mom in Utah," she said. "I'm just here visiting my dad."

"Well, how do you two get along?"

Her face fell a bit. "He started drinking when Mom left. He's always mad about something nowadays. I hate it because that means he's always drunk."

"So, why do you come down here to see him?" I asked.

"Because I miss him, despite it all."

An hour or so went by, and we finished our refreshments. I looked down at my watch, and I couldn't believe it was already after midnight.

"Are your friends waiting for you?" I asked.

"No," she smiled. "I was actually hoping you could give me a ride home."

This is going better than I planned.

"Of course, I'll take you home. Where do you live?"

"Off Bonanza and Lamb. Is that too far? I can still call my girl-friend and —"

"No, it's no problem!" I said a little too eagerly. "The longer ride just gives me more time to spend with you."

I took my time driving her home. Her arms wrapped around me felt just right, and I could get used to that feeling real quick. When we stopped at a red light on Bonanza, she reached up and pulled my head around to hers. I turned around in my seat as far as I could, and our lips met for the first time.

Our first kiss had traffic stopped. Horns blared at us to move after the light turned green, but we didn't care. Cars inched themselves around us as we sat in the middle of the lane, kissing. For the moment, I forgot where I was and got lost in her arms. I got dizzy from the smell of her neck and pulled her in closer.

Suddenly, the moment was broken as I felt the bike falling over. I quickly turned and grabbed the handlebars. I pulled the bike back upright, and we both started laughing.

I popped my Sportster down into first gear, and we continued our journey. A few minutes later, we were at her dad's place. I flipped the kickstand out and turned off the bike. We fell into each other's arms.

I slowly kissed her neck as she made tiny satisfied sighs and made my way up to her open mouth. My mind was telling me that things were moving way too fast, but my heart was telling me how right this felt. I had kissed many girls before, but none of them tasted like this.

I ran my hand up the nape of her neck and into her hair. My fingers massaged her scalp as I cupped her head with the palm of my hand. She wound her body around mine and held my face between her hands. I didn't think we were going to be able to stop, but we had to come up for air.

"I want you to come in with me," she said. "It's late, and my dad might be mad."

"How am I going to make any difference?"

"If you're there, he may not get as mad," she pleaded. "Walk in with me, please."

"Don't you think that if I walk in, it may make things worse?"

She stood there, her eyes so sweet and wide as she looked imploringly into mine. I knew I'd never be able to say no to that face.

"Lead the way."

We made our way up the lawn to the front porch, where she unlocked the door. I followed her inside to see a huge, bearded man reclined on the couch with a beer in one hand and cigar in the other. I moved in closer behind her and that's when the shit hit the fan.

"Do you know what time it is? Where the hell have you been all night? And who the fuck is that?"

"Dad, you knew I was going out with Lisa tonight," she said calmly, as if she were talking to an agitated grizzly. "Then I met Rick, and he took me out to eat. We just lost track of time, Daddy. I'm sorry."

"You're barely 17 years old, young lady. You can't afford to lose track of time."

My heart plummeted into my stomach. She's only 17 years old, and I'm standing here in front of her drunk father, probably with a couple of blossoming hickeys. *17? Jesus Christ!*

"You're grounded for the rest of the time you are here!" he shouted. "Get to your room!"

Her dad turned his glower to me.

"You best get the hell out of my house."

At that point, I was more than willing to oblige, but before I could say a word, Jackie jumped in.

"If he leaves, I'm going with him!"

"No, Jackie," I said, backing to the door, holding her gaze. "It's cool. I'll talk to you later."

"No, take me with you! I'm not staying here!"

"Oh, really?" the grizzly growled. "Well, we'll just see about that."

He got to his feet and stumbled past us down the hallway to the bedroom. I heard the distinctive ratchet sound of shells being fed into the chamber of a shotgun.

"Oh my God," she said with a look of horror. "He's loading his gun!"

"No shit!" I said. "Sorry Jackie, but I'm out of here!"

I turned and ran out the door. Even though I had some training in martial arts, I knew the only defense against a drunk, shotgun-wielding father was to run.

My Harley looked as if it were a mile away. I ran as fast as I could, almost falling as I slid in the grass when I got to my bike. I jumped onto the bike, my ears straining for a hammer click. I pumped the pedal up with my right leg and was ready to come down hard on it when Jackie's hand clasped onto my forearm.

"Jackie, what are you doing?"

"Take me with you Rick, please!"

She was terrified, and I could see the tears welling in her eyes. I kicked down hard on the pedal, and I prayed my bike would start.

With a loud roar, my engine came to life and idled between my legs, ready to go. I sat on my bike and looked deeply into her tear-filled eyes. There was no way I could leave her. I held my hand out, and she smiled in relief. She grabbed my hand and pulled herself onto the seat.

"Hold on," I said.

I found first gear and punched it. I was still waiting to hear a shotgun blast coming at us, but all I heard was my Harley's pipes screaming through each gear.

When we pulled up in front of my studio apartment about 20 minutes later, my heart was still racing.

"Seventeen?!" I yelled as we walked inside. "You're 17? Are you kidding me?"

"What difference does that make?" she asked defensively. "What, I'm not good enough for you anymore?"

"Jackie, you're a minor," I explained emphatically. "You're what people refer to as 'jail-bait'. Understand?"

She paused. "Look me in the eyes and tell me that matters to you." She crossed the room and pushed herself into my face. "Tell me it matters, go ahead. Do you want me to leave?" She emphasized each word of her question and searched my eyes.

How could I feel this much for a girl in just one night? I looked into her eyes and my first thought was to kiss her lips, but I stopped myself.

"So, what's the plan now?" I asked, partly to myself.

I realized that I was pacing, so I made myself sit down on the couch. She walked over to the door and stood facing it. I thought she was going to leave, but then she slowly turned towards me and wiped her eyes.

"I need to go back to Utah," she said. "I need to talk to my mom. Will you take me?"

"No, Jackie," I shook my head. "For more than one reason."

"You know, Rick," she said with an edge to her voice. "If I hadn't met you, I wouldn't be in this fix."

"Come on, Jackie. That's not fair, and you know it."

She turned her back to me again and, with her forehead pressed against the door, she apologized.

"I'm sorry, you're right. I shouldn't have said that. I just don't know what to do."

"How about a bus ticket back home?" I asked gently. "I'll take you to the bus station, if you want."

"You want me to take the bus home? You know what? This is where you and I end!" She shouted.

I didn't like the sound of those words, but I knew this was how it had to be.

"What do you want me to do, baby?" I really didn't know. She was 17, and I didn't want to go to jail.

"Nothing," she sighed, her anger vanishing as quickly as it had flared. "I'm just going to call my mom. When she finds out what my dad did, she'll drive right out here and get me."

"It sounds like you have a great mom."

"I do." She smiled. "Do you have a phone I could use? I need to call Lisa to pick me up."

She made the call to her girlfriend first, and then she called her mom in

Utah. Her mom calmed her down and said she would pick her up at Lisa's house first thing in the morning.

We sat and talked about what had happened and actually had a good laugh over it. There were times when the conversation stopped, and we just stared at each other in silence. I really wanted her to stay in Vegas, but I knew that wasn't going to happen with her dad wanting to shoot me. I took her hands into mine and stared into her eyes. Jackie finally broke the silence.

"Rick …" she paused. "I think I —"

She was interrupted by a loud knock at the door. She reluctantly let my hands go and walked to the door. It was Lisa, and she was in a hurry.

"Goodbye, Rick," Jackie said. "I bet I'm going to miss you."

We laughed sadly, but it felt good to see her smile. I walked over and hugged her.

"I bet I'm going to miss you too."

She turned and walked out without looking back. I watched them drive away before slowly closing the door and putting my back to it for a few moments to think. I made my way to the sofa bed and sat on the edge. I kicked off my boots and laid back. I didn't realize how tired I was until my head hit the pillow. I closed my eyes and thought, "Wow, I can't believe my bike started on the first kick tonight."

STOLEN STEEL

The summer of '71 had come to an end, and winter was creeping in. Sitting on Fremont Street was becoming a less frequent event for us as we sought out the warmth of the nightclubs, but riding our Harleys was in our blood. We rode rain or shine, in the desert heat or the bitter cold. We didn't care.

My Sportster turned out to be very temperamental, thought. She was a '71 XLCH kick start Sportster 900cc with a Tillotson racing carb that was very sensitive to temperature, altitude, and (as I believe) even humidity changes. But regardless of the weather, she had her own personality and would start only when she wanted, and it would sometimes drive me totally crazy.

She usually started after a few kicks if I was careful with the choke and throttle. But then there were times I would kick her repeatedly, and she'd still sit there, silent and stubborn.

I hated her when she wouldn't start and loved her when she did. She was unpredictable, but I never once thought about selling her. It was a love/hate relationship, and I wasn't giving up on my Harley. She could be a headache, but she was my headache.

I worked swing shift at the base and graveyard shift at the Mint Hotel Downtown. I had weekends off from the base, so I hung out at the nightclubs on weekends before work, valet parking cars for some extra cash and something to do.

I lived downtown on 6th Street in a studio apartment, which was close to work at the Mint Hotel. I chose to live off base, and this place was as good as any for right now. I pulled into my parking space and unlocked the heavy-duty chain I had wrapped around a wooden parking curb. I pulled it through my front wheel and reattached the lock.

I walked through the gate to my first-floor patio and unlocked the sliding glass door. After about 40 minutes, I was done with my shower and ready to head for work. I locked the sliding glass door and stepped out onto the walkway from my patio into the cool November night air.

I started looking for my bike as I walked down the narrow pathway. My space was just a little left of the walkway and I could usually spot it by the time I was halfway down. As I got closer, I started looking for the front wheel of my bike to appear around the corner of the fence.

The closer I got, the bigger the knot in my stomach became. She didn't seem to be there.

I vehemently denied what my instincts were telling me was true. My pace quickened involuntarily, and I reached the end of the walkway, stopping dead in my tracks.

All that was left lying in my parking space was a broken chain. The world stopped, and I heard nothing but my own heart thudding loudly in my ears. I ran over to my spot and picked up the chain. It felt cold and lifeless in my hands as I stared at the cut links.

I looked down the alley, but it was dark and empty. I threw the chain down and ran through the parking lot to the street.

It, too, was dark and empty. My head started spinning to the point that I felt like I was going to be sick. I looked back down at the broken chain, curled up like a chrome snake on the pavement. I stood there for the longest time in disbelief, willing my bike back into its spot. I wasn't sure what I should do. All I could think about was finding the asshole who stole my Harley.

I went back into the apartment and called the cops. I wanted them to come down right away and treat my parking space like a crime scene. I needed them to hunt down the thieves and bring them to justice, but they said that it wasn't going to happen. They wanted me to come down to the station and file a report, and they'd see what they could do.

I slammed the phone down and picked it back up to call work. I told my boss, Gary, what had happened and that I wouldn't be in tonight. I jumped into my 1961 Chevy Impala and headed for the police station.

A bored receptionist smacking gum gave me a clipboard and a pen and told me to fill out the report and contact my insurance company. No one at the police station seemed even the least bit interested that a piece of my heart and soul had been ripped from my life with nothing but a broken chain left in its wake.

I made up my mind that I didn't need anyone — not the cops, not the detectives, not anyone.

I was going to find my bike and the thief that stole it, and I was going to tear him apart.

Returning home felt surreal. I stood in the spot and went over and over in my head what had happened. How could they have stolen it? I was only gone for 40 minutes or so. Had they been watching me? Was it someone I knew? All at once, it hit me and the reality of it set in — she was gone.

The next morning, I contacted my insurance company. They said there was a 30-day waiting period on stolen property to see if the police could come up with anything. I knew that wasn't going to happen, so I was going to be without a Harley for the next month. To a 23-year-old, that was a lifetime.

I sat alone in my studio apartment many nights when I would be normally out at the clubs. Having my Sportster stolen from me ripped out a part of my sanity. I was always mad about something, even if it wasn't related to my bike. A part of my soul was gone, and I was mad at the world.

I stayed away from the Harley shop for the first 3 weeks, which was harder than I expected. On the fourth week, I finally gave in and went down to see RR and what kind of inventory he had on the showroom floor.

I couldn't believe my eyes. There on the showroom floor sat a brand new 1972 Harley Sportster XLH, and it was blue, just like mine. It looked a lot like my '71 XLCH, but this one was an electric start with a new 1000cc motor with a Bendix carb. I had to have it.

I had found my next love, but this time, she was even better. No more kick-starting for this boy. I gave RR $500 to hold it for me, and a week later, I was rolling her out the door. Everything in life felt so much better; food tasted better, the air smelled like flowers, and I could feel the wind in my hair again. I didn't realize that being without a Harley for so long after owning one would depress me so much. The pain from having my Harley stolen right out from under my nose left me with a constant sick feeling in my gut.

I loved my new Sportster but still ached for the old one. It was like an open wound that just wouldn't scab. I needed revenge, and I was going to have it. This town wasn't as big as most people think, and I already knew most of the bikers that hung out on Fremont Street. That only left a few of the clubs that were scattered across the valley.

It had to be one of them.

Sheriff Ralph Lamb hated the biker clubs and always put the heat on them whenever possible, so they usually kept to themselves, and I didn't know much about them. But I needed to meet a couple of the members and see if I could get some information on my stolen bike. How could I have known how drastically this would alter my life course?

I spent my weekends hanging out at the dive bars I had seen club members frequent. After some time, a back-patched biker came in alone and ordered a beer a few stools away from where I was perched. He sat there for a while, bullshitting with the bartender, an older guy who had definitely seen better days. The biker was about my age and seemed like the right guy to talk to.

The patch on his vest transfixed me. It was barbaric and powerful; it made a bold statement about the man who wore it. In fact, it made such a bold statement that it actually made it hard to just walk up and start a conversation.

After a while, the biker got up and made his way toward the restroom.

Only then did I notice the three gnarly-looking dudes sitting in the corner. I had been so focused on the biker that I hadn't given them any notice. As the door swung shut behind the biker from the bar, the three guys stood up and walked towards the restroom, smiling devilishly and hyping each other up.

"The bathroom is occupied," the bartender said sternly, as aware of the situation as I was.

One of the thugs shoved a finger in his direction and growled, "If you know what's good for you, old man, you'll mind your own business."

One of the others glared at me and said, "That goes for you, too."

Satisfied with their threats, the three of them disappeared into the restroom.

"Son of a bitch," the bartender mumbled as he pulled out a broken pool stick from behind the counter. His hands were shaking as he started walking out from behind the bar.

"Hey," I said reassuringly. "Don't worry, I got this."

I walked over and took the pool cue from his hands, asking, "Is that guy a friend of yours?"

"Yeah, he's one of my regulars and a good guy."

"Then you won't mind if I check in on him." I raised my brows meaningfully.

"Please," he said, understanding. "Be my guest."

With a tight grip on my make-shift weapon, I kicked open the restroom door.

A couple steps into the john revealed two guys holding the biker up while the third guy was busy punching him out. When his two buddies turned to look wide-eyed at me and my stake, the slugger turned to see who had just kicked open the door.

"This has nothing to do with you, asshole," he said. "You best turn around and get the fuck out of here."

He didn't wait long to see if I'd get the hint before striding cockily toward me. I came up with the fat end of the pool cue and jabbed it heavily into his forehead. He dropped like a lifeless ragdoll to the grungy tile floor.

Seeing their pal crumple to the floor, the other two dudes let their guard down just long enough for the biker to break loose and start swinging. He kneed the first dude in the crotch and shoved him head first in my direction. I cracked him on top of the skull as he stumbled toward me, sending him to join his buddy on the floor. I looked up and the biker was punching the last dude without mercy. I had never seen that much blood come from someone's face.

With the three assholes moaning at our feet, the biker turned to me.

"You OK, man?" he asked, rubbing the trickle of blood oozing from a gash in his cheek.

"Yeah, I'm fine, but I don't think we'll be shooting pool with this stick anytime soon." I held it up where its two halves hung from a sliver. "How about you? You good?"

He gingerly held a hand to his ribs and grimaced before giving me a crooked smile.

"Yeah, I'm OK," he answered. "You know, that was my favorite stick."

"You might say I broke it in for you," I laughed. "Did you know these turkeys?" I nudged one in the neck with my boot.

"Turkeys? I like that," the biker said. "No, this came out of nowhere."

One of the dudes tried to get up, but the biker sent him back to the floor with a heavy kick to the kidney.

I tossed the stick to the floor, and we walked out of the restroom. The bartender greeted us with a huge smile and a couple shots of Crown, on the house. We slammed the shots and introduced ourselves more properly.

"I'm Hiney," said the biker. "And you are?"

"I'm Rick, nice meeting you."

Hiney nodded and turned to the bartender. "Hal, you should call an ambulance for those guys to cover your ass. You don't know us, right?"

"You got it, man," said the bartender. "Fuck those guys."

Hiney and I walked out of the bar together. He stopped in his tracks and stared, mouth agape at my Harley.

"You ride, man?"

"It's my life! Where are we headed?"

Hiney swung his leg over his bike and said, "Better be damn sure you want to follow me. You'll have to do more than just prove yourself to me."

"Of course! Lead the way."

We gunned our Harleys and popped the clutches, sending us flying out of the parking lot of the Backstreet Tavern. My adrenaline was pumping like mad. I still couldn't keep my eyes off Hiney's patch as we raced through the Vegas valley to the east side of town. I wondered what it would be like to be a patch holder and figured I was on my way to find out.

We were out by Nellis Air Force Base, and after going down some side streets, we pulled onto a long dirt driveway. We pulled up in front of what I figured was Hiney's house and shut down our bikes. Other than a group of Mulberry trees surrounding the house, the area was all desert. Sunrise Mountain was on the horizon, and for a long stretch there was no sign of civilization.

I followed Hiney into the house and was immediately greeted by three other club members who were working on a Panhead's motor. One of the wrencher-wielders stood up and pointed at me.

"Who's the stray dog?"

"Hey man, this guy just saved my ass from a bunch of turkeys at the bar."

"Is that a fact?" another of them said. "Turkeys, huh? So, who the fuck is *this turkey,* and why did you bring him to the club house?"

"I brought him here because I think he's good people. He had my back when the chips were down, and we could use more people like him around."

"Well, I don't like him. He's gotta leave."

"Look, Stroker," Hiney said a little more forcefully. "I'm vouching for him, so he stays."

"You don't have to vouch for me, Hiney," I said, stepping forward. "I'm not looking for any favors."

I looked over at the guy called Stroker, who was staring at me with a rubber mallet in his hand. He narrowed his eyes and turned to Hiney then slowly back to me. "Well, what do you want?"

I grinned confidently. "What do I want? I want to join up with you guys."

TO BE CONTINUED . . .

Rotten Ralph

Lil' Mike

Norton

Greg and Vicki

Camping at Mount Charleston with Mario, Bear, Rotten Ralph, and Lew

Hiney and Ann

Doc and Big Mike

Bear and Baron

Big Mike

Hiney

Baby Huey

Meeting up for the run to Ash Springs

Ash Springs run

Gloria on the set of "The Gauntlet"

Clint directing us on the set

Filming "The Gauntlet" with Clint

Me with my 1968 FLH
bought from Cecil

My 1968 FLH at Red
Rock Canyon

The Stolen Steel: 1971
XLCH Harley Sportster

Look for the thrilling conclusion to
Turk's quest for retribution in

SIN CITY
RETRIBUTION

A GAME CALLED
REVENGE

Coming Soon!

ABOUT THE AUTHOR

Rick Hart moved to Las Vegas from Virginia in 1969 while in the U.S. Air Force. After leaving the military, Rick attained a Fourth Degree Black Belt in Shorin Ryu Karate and became a Five Star PADI Scuba Diver. Rick also received two degrees from the Clark County Community College and now works at a major resort hotel on the Las Vegas Strip. Rick loves spending time with his five kids, 12 grandkids, three great-grandchildren, and his Boo-Doggy. He enjoys riding his Harley as much as always through the mountains that surround the Las Vegas valley.

31313879R00104